P9-ARI-659

737.4
W37

FREE PUBLIC LIBRARY

Wear, Ted G.

Coin collecting in a nutshell

# WITHDRAWN

No longer the property of the
Boston Public Library.
Sale of this material benefits the Library.

WITHDRAWN
No longer the property of the
Boston Public Library.
Sale of this material benefits the Library

COIN COLLECTING *in a Nutshell*

# COIN
# COLLECTING
## *in a Nutshell*

TED G. WEAR

1963
*Doubleday & Company, Inc.*
*Garden City, New York*

CJ89
.N4

LIBRARY OF CONGRESS CATALOG CARD NUMBER 63-16630
COPYRIGHT © 1963 BY TED G. WEAR
ALL RIGHTS RESERVED
PRINTED IN THE UNITED STATES OF AMERICA
FIRST EDITION

# CONTENTS

## LIST OF ILLUSTRATIONS

### Following page 72

Unchanged for 50 years—the Lincoln cent.
Sharper's Delight—1833 nickel, with no "cents."
This was Black Diamond.
Liberty becomes modest.

### RECOGNIZE THESE COINS?

Columbian Exposition half dollar.
Isabella quarter dollar.
George Washington on a dollar.

### A MINT IS STARTED

From Martha's Silverware? Half disme of 1792.
You were expected to know value—dime and half dime.
Early eagles were sometimes skinny.
Portrait of Peter, the mint eagle.

### THREE CLASSIFICATIONS

*Impossible*—Three early U.S. half dollars.
*Unlikely*—Seated Liberty, Barber Halves.
*Possible*—Walking Liberty, Franklin Halves.

### UNFAMILIAR U. S. COINS

Half cent and large cent.
Two-cent piece of 1864.
Three-cents—of nickel or silver.
That confusing 20-cent piece.

### UNUSUAL U. S. COINS

Easy to lose—dollars of gold.
Stella—the high-priced lady.
The "Poor Relation"—$3 gold.
Silver dollars for the Orient.

COIN COLLECTING *in a Nutshell*

# CHAPTER ONE

## *So You've Got Some Old Coins!*

# SO YOU'VE GOT SOME OLD COINS!

So you've got some old coins!

Well now, that's just fine.

So what are you going to do with those old coins?

What *can* you do with them? There are four courses of action open to you.

You can—
1. Spend 'em.
2. Save 'em.
3. Give 'em away.
4. Sell 'em.

Let's examine each possibility.

1. *No matter how old, if they are United States coins, you can spend them.* Of course, the blonde beauty in the box office may take a dim view of that 1825 half dollar— she may even decline to accept it. But it's worth every one of the 50 cents called for. The merchant collecting sales tax may object somewhat when you put down a half-cent copper of 1809 to pay out the exact tax percentage. And he may not like it too much when you offer a 3-cent silver piece (1851) and a 2-cent copper (1864) in payment for that pack of gum. But every one of those old coins is as full legal tender as the day it was issued by the U. S. Mint.

2. *If you decide to save them, you may gain considerably in the long run.* After you study them, understand their place in United States history, learn what makes them valuable, you may decide to use them as a basis for a coin collection of your own. Such a course of action, if it suits

your temperament and pocketbook, may appear costly at first because, after all, you can't get old and valuable coins at face value today. But if you do become a serious collector of fine old coins, it probably will pay off handsomely, not only in personal pleasure, but in future dollars and cents.

3. *If you decide to give them away, present them to some youngster who'll enjoy them thoroughly—at least for a time.* It is indeed remarkable how those little discs of metal called money can fascinate a boy or girl. The coins may be from foreign countries and of no particular value to a United States coin collector. This almost never detracts from their attractiveness to the young accumulator. That they represent value to someone somewhere in the world is quite enough—for the present, at least.

4. *The fourth and final course of action is to sell them.*

If you're like most Americans, you're not the least bit interested in the appearance of the coins (except that they "look old"); you couldn't care less about why they were issued or who designed them. You want the answer to just one brusque question: "How much are they worth?"

That's not an easy question to answer. It's something like: "I've got an old automobile—what's it worth?" Now, you may have a genuine antique auto almost as bright as the day it came from the maker. Or you may have a broken-down car that's only a cough and a gasp from the scrap pile. How much is each "old automobile" worth?

So it goes with coins. One may be ready for the junk heap, another a classic that deserves an honored place among the best. To the average person, unschooled in the world of numismatics (the science of coins and medals), they have one thing in common—they're "old." But age alone doesn't bring value to a coin, any more than it makes an old auto desirable.

There's another question that keeps cropping up: "How old must a coin be to be valuable?"

While not quite the same as the classic riddle, "How old is Ann?" it's even more difficult to answer. An ancient Roman coin in mediocre condition may be worth only a dollar or so, even though it is more than 2,000 years old. At the other extreme, a certain American cent, not yet 50 years old, will bring several hundred dollars if it's in Uncirculated condition—as new as the day it came from the mint. The factors involved aren't too difficult to understand. There are three, and they are:

1. In the United States there are thousands of collectors, young and old, who are trying to put together sets of Lincoln cents. They create a continuing demand for certain coins to complete the series. In contrast, there are far fewer American collectors of ancient Roman coins. The demand for a "key" Lincoln cent (the one needed to complete the set) raises the going price far above its face value. Similarly, the lack of demand for mediocre ancient coins makes them almost unsalable. Thus, demand is probably the most important factor in determining how much a coin is worth.

2. Almost everyone prefers a brand new article to one that's nearly worn out—whether it's a motor car, a fur coat or a kitchen stove. The mint-new Lincoln cent struck at Denver in 1914 is most desirable to the collector of small cents. The worn bronze coin of a Roman emperor is not aesthetically pleasing nor is it particularly desirable to the person who collects the coins of such emperors. And, since there are available today those same coins in a beautiful state of preservation (at more money, of course), why settle for less? Thus, the condition of a coin could be said to be the second most important consideration in valuing a coin.

3. How many of a certain type of coin were struck in a stated year? This question may have a definite bearing on the value of that coin. And a second question may have to

be given an answer, even if it's only approximate: How many have survived and are available today? For example, the then-new U. S. Mint reported that it struck only 7,776 silver dollars in the year 1797. How many are in existence today? No one can be absolutely certain, but it has been estimated that about 4 per cent may have survived in all conditions. If this estimate is accurate there may be some 311 of the 1797-dated United States silver dollars available to the collector of early silver dollars.

It is small wonder then that a 1797 United States dollar today has a market value ranging from under $100 for a specimen in "Good" condition to over $1,000 for one in "Uncirculated."

At the other end of the comparison, in the years 1944 and 1945, the U. S. Mint at Philadelphia struck over a billion Lincoln cents each year! In a hundred years or so, those cents, if still bright and uncirculated, may be worth considerably more than face value. But they are not worth much today—nor will they be tomorrow.

The three elements which today are the principal factors in determining a coin's value may be stated thus:

1. Demand.
2. Condition.
3. Number available.

# CHAPTER TWO

## The Value of
## a Coin

# THE VALUE OF A COIN

About those old coins you have—how did you happen to get them? Did you find them in the attic—in that old Saratoga trunk that once belonged to your great-grandfather?

They may have considerable value—*if* your ancestor was a coin collector who knew what he was doing.

They may be fairly valuable if he made a practice of putting away any bright new coins as they came his way in change.

But, if your great-grandmother was the one who accumulated (rather than collected) the coins—mostly because they looked old—they probably will have some but not a great deal of value.

How do you find out how much your old coins are actually worth? Well, there are two types of catalogs available which will help you—and you can buy either or both. One catalog purports to tell you how much a dealer will pay you for a specific coin. Its prices are usually on the definitely conservative side. The other catalog tells you how much a dealer will charge you for that same coin. Somewhere between the two figures will be about what you may expect to realize from the sale of that coin.

In the coin-collecting business, condition is a most important consideration. A coin in an absolute mint state of perfection may be worth as much as a hundred dollars or more. That same coin, well-worn and in what would be graded as "Good" condition, may be worth only 25 or 50 cents.

And how do you, an absolute amateur, determine the

condition of a coin? It's not impossible, but it may take some
months for you to become an expert on the subject. Unless
you plan to become a genuine, dyed-in-the-wool collector,
you don't want to spend that much time.

So you decide to take them around to some dealers and
see what they'll offer you for your old coins. But there are
some dangers in that course of action. There are, to be sure,
highly reputable dealers who would never dream of taking
advantage of your ignorance; others are less ethical. But
you plan to get several offers on your coins.

You start out. The first dealer, if he's at all interested,
asks how much you want for your coins. You don't know
—so you ask for an offer. He repeats: "How much do you
want for the lot?" When you decline to state a price
(mostly because you haven't any idea of their worth), he
regrets his inability to make an offer.

You may wonder why he declines to give you any estimate of the worth of your old coins. It's not too difficult
to understand. You're asking him, in effect, to appraise your
coins without charge—to go out on a limb so that other dealers can snipe at his offer.

He knows that, if he's the first dealer you've talked to,
you may decide to shop around until you find another
dealer who will give you a little bit over his offer—it may be
only 50 cents or a dollar. The coin business today is quite
competitive, and no dealer likes to lose out to another over
a matter of pennies. They may be important to you; they
irritate the dealer.

Until you have some inkling of the coins' worth, you probably won't have any idea how much to ask.

You may wonder: Is the dealer being fair to you? In almost any other business involving antiques, a dealer will
usually make an offer. But that old bureau or antique table,
which the dealer made his bid on, can't be toted too easily.

You may hesitate to shop around—to try another dealer or two.

You've probably made up your mind as to about what it's worth. You have decided that this or that antique dealer is reputable. So you've taken your antique to his shop. And you'll probably accept his offer if he approximates your estimate. He may even agree to raise it a bit to the amount you think your table or chest of drawers is worth.

But in the coin business, it is all too simple merely to stuff your coins back into the envelope or old cigar box and walk out to try another shop. The dealer knows this—and it makes him reluctant to quote a figure. If he's the first or second dealer you've visited, he knows that his bid, no matter how generous, won't be acceptable to you, for you're still shopping around.

So what's your best bet? Determine as best you can a reputable dealer who will appraise your coins—for a fee, of course. Ask him to make the appraisal on their value to him, as a dealer. While the percentage fee is slightly higher on this type appraisal, you will be getting not only an expert's statement as to value, but a firm offer to buy.

You may be shocked at the lowness of the appraisal figure, or delighted by its size. But you'll be certain of one thing: the next reputable dealer, down the street or across town, won't vary more than a percentage point or two from that honestly-appraised price.

A word of caution: Before you take off on your selling trip, don't attempt to improve on the appearance of your coins. They may look dull; don't attempt to shine them. Always remember that your best-intentioned efforts cannot improve the coin's value one bit. Instead, you may damage it and actually lower its grade and value materially.

Never try to clean a coin in any way if you plan to sell it. The buyer, whether he's a dealer or collector, does not object to a dull-appearing coin; in fact, this evidence of age, known as patina in some cases, is most desirable.

Let's look in on a coin dealer as he encounters a man who has a shiny coin he'd like to sell. Only someone has "played with the coin" and attempted to cover up the aging and wear and tear that come naturally to everything—coins as well as humans.

"I got something good I want to show you."

There was the air of the gambler about the man. His suit was just a bit too sharp, his manner too breezy. The dealer recognized the type and prepared to take the whole thing in stride.

From an inside pocket, the man took a folded bit of paper. Elaborately he opened it. The dealer indicated a velvet-covered tray and the man ceremoniously placed the gold dollar on it.

"Know what that is?" he demanded.

"Of course. It's a gold dollar," answered the dealer patiently.

"Ever see one brighter and shinier? It's just like it came from the mint. Notice the date—it's a good one—1870. Know how many gold dollars were made that year?"

The dealer gave a tired smile.

"Offhand, I don't recall the exact mint figures for that year."

"They turned out 6,300 of these gold dollars in 1870—just exactly 6,300—not one more." The visitor paused. The dealer didn't appear impressed. Finally, he said:

"So?"

"So what'll you give me for that brand new dollar?"

"In the first place," began the dealer, "the coin is not brand new."

"Why!" the man exploded. "It's as bright and shiny as it ever was."

"Maybe it looks that way to you."

"It has a very high catalog value—$100 in Uncirculated —and over $200 in Proof. Maybe this is a Proof, huh?"

"It's not a Proof and it certainly isn't Uncirculated now."

"How can you tell?"

"Many ways; but the easiest is simply by the amount of wear on the coin. The high points are entirely smooth, and——"

The man interrupted:

"You mean, I got stuck? I didn't get a bargain? The fellow who sold it to me said it was a darn good coin."

"It was—once. I don't know what you paid for it, but——"

"I gave this fellow $50 for it."

"Well, I'm afraid I'd have trouble selling it for more than $5."

The man looked down at his gold dollar, then picked it up.

"But tell me—how come it looks so brand new?"

"Someone buffed it—probably used jeweler's rouge on it. Trying to make it look young again, they ruined it."

"Oh, well," said the man, as he pocketed the coin, "guess I better stick to horses—you're always fairly sure how old they are."

So, if your coins look a little old and dirty, leave them that way.

Among the do's and don'ts you should follow if you want full value from your coins:

Don't use an eraser to brighten a silver coin. Sure, it makes it look shinier, but that shine won't fool any coin expert into thinking your coin is fresh from the mint.

Leave copper coins as you find them. A household cleanser, while it will brighten copper coins and make them shine, gives them an unnatural color that fools no one and even makes them undesirable to many.

Avoid jeweler's rouge and the buffing wheel as you would the plague. They'll make the worn spots even more prominent.

If eventually you should become a coin collector and have a certain piece you think might be improved by careful cleaning, don't try to do it yourself. Take it to an expert who can advise whether the coin can be cleaned successfully, whether its value will be improved thereby, and how much the job will cost you.

# CHAPTER THREE

# A Brief Guide
# to Condition

# A BRIEF GUIDE TO CONDITION

The little old lady came into the coin shop. Carefully she opened her handbag and extracted a large well-worn copper cent. Then she announced:

"I'm sure this old penny is very valuable. It's been in my family for more than a hundred years. It's very old. Why, it's so old, even the date is worn off."

It was the dealer's unpleasant task to tell her that her dateless coin was worthless—at least, that it was without numismatic value. Not only was the date long since gone from the coin, it was so worn that even the type was not clear.

Almost without exception, a dateless coin is valueless to the dealer and to the collector. An exception might be found in the 1796 United States silver quarter dollar. This quarter, first issued by the U. S. Mint, was of a particular pattern and was struck in the year 1796 only. So, if the type could be made out, if the portrait was identifiable, it would have some value over and above its face of 25 cents.

To the collector, such a coin would be a "space filler"—a legitimate piece of metal to fit properly in his 25-cent collection until he could find or was able to afford a better specimen. While a quarter of 1796 in "Fine" condition will bring many hundreds of dollars, such a dateless and thoroughly worn but identifiable coin probably would be worth only a few dollars.

Since it is condition that's so important in determining coin values, let's try to understand something about coin grading. An understandable comparison might be made by matching coins and motor cars. This comparison will go something as follows:

| COIN CONDITION | MOTOR CAR CONDITION |
|---|---|
| *Gem Uncirculated* | Brand new. You go to the factory and buy it—no chance for anything to have happened to it—it's right off the assembly line. |
| *Uncirculated* | Also brand new, but you go to your dealer's showroom for delivery. It may have been transported on one of those truck trailers and some dust and weather may have had their effect. These minute signs of handling may be compared to the "bag scratches" often found on absolutely Uncirculated coins. Such coins, sealed in canvas bags for transport, have been jostled against each other and they've picked up just enough tiny dents and scratches to have lost the rating of "Gem." |
| *Extremely Fine* | Once around the block. No accidents, a quite uneventful journey. But, as anyone knows who's ever bought a new car, its original value has been materially depreciated. Similarly, the Extremely Fine coin may have been in circulation only a day or so (once around the block), but the full mint bloom has faded. |
| *Very Fine* | A few weeks old, maybe left out overnight in a rainstorm or two. Tires aren't quite as fresh and the finish hasn't quite the same original luster. But there are no dents showing and the motor purrs as smoothly as ever. |
| *Fine* | Excellent mechanical condition, maybe a scratch or two here and there, but most desirable in appearance. Tires are starting to show wear and the chrome hints at some future rustiness. |

| COIN CONDITION | MOTOR CAR CONDITION |
|---|---|
| *Very Good* | Still desirable in general, but perhaps hailstones have dented the roof somewhat. There's no doubt about the make or year or model. Considerable tire tread wear, but a lot of mileage left. |
| *Good* | Lots of wear showing, but still good, dependable transportation. All original parts in place and functioning. Tires almost worn smooth but not dangerously so. Quite acceptable as a second car or for those whose budget is limited. |
| *Fair* | Has four wheels, a motor and that's about all. Not desirable at all unless it's of some rare vintage year. |
| *Poor* | Where's the nearest scrap heap? |

If you can visualize the life cycle of a motor car from the day it emerges bright and shiny from the factory until it's ready for the junkyard, you'll have a fairly good idea of the life cycle of the average American coin.

United States proof coins—those hydraulically struck from specially polished dies—which now are issued each year primarily for coin-collecting purposes, might be compared to the custom-built motor car. The amount of handwork involved differs greatly, but that's the closest comparison possible, distant though it may be.

While the condition of a motor car can be improved by the installation of a new motor or the replacement of worn-out tires with new ones, the same cannot be done successfully with coins. If a coin's rim is seriously dented, it cannot be replaced like a car's fender, or even straightened out. If the face of Liberty is almost obliterated, no surgery will enable you to lift it out and put in a new one.

As mentioned previously, another factor that will have a

bearing on the value of your United States coins is the total
number minted in any year.

It stands to reason that a bronze cent of which only
852,000 were struck (and this back in 1877) should have
considerably more value than a cent of 1944, when the com-
bined output of the three United States mints totaled more
than 2 billion coppers. The smallest 1944 production was
from the San Francisco mint, which issued a total of more
than 252 million of the copper coins—quite a contrast to the
skimpy 852,000 of some 67 years earlier.

But the number minted isn't always a safe and certain
guide. Collector-demand plays a very large part in the final
determination of what a coin is worth. For some unex-
plained reason (perhaps because it's so easy and inexpensive to get started collecting them), the small cents of the
United States long have enjoyed tremendous popularity
with collectors of almost all ages. And, with such widespread demand and a limited number of certain cents, the
collector who wants to complete his date set has to pay
higher and higher prices for certain dates.

One example of this tremendous demand for the small
cent is that same 1877 Indian Head cent mentioned earlier.
The U. S. Mint that year turned out 852,000 such cents.
The same year, the mint issued a total of 397,670 $20 gold
pieces—less than half the number of cents.

If the Uncirculated Indian Head cent of 1877 catalogs at
$400 (it may be higher any minute now), that is 40,000
times its face value of one cent. Thus, an 1877 $20 gold
piece, less than half as common as the cent, *ought* to be
worth at least 40,000 *its* face value, or $800,000. But, alas,
it is not!

Demand far outstrips supply in the case of the 1-cent
piece; there are plenty of $20 gold pieces to go around. So,
in the same catalog listing the 1877 cent at $400, you'll find
the 1877 Uncirculated $20 gold coin listed at a mere $95.

Similarly, in 1914, the U. S. Mint at Denver turned out 1,193,000 bronze cents, all duly marked with the "D" mint letter. The same year, 448,000 $2.50 gold pieces were issued—less than half as many.

While the Uncirculated 1914-D cent was quoted at around $400, the twice-as-scarce $2.50 in gold had a catalog quotation of a mere $35 in Uncirculated condition.

Thus, collector-demand continues to play hob with the best-laid statistics.

CHAPTER FOUR

# Values That Go Up
# —and Up!

# VALUES THAT GO UP—AND UP!

In the last 15 years or so, the prices of many coins have risen—some slightly, some spectacularly—and some prices have gone down.

Which ones may be expected to rise in the future is almost anybody's guess. The public (and that includes those who collect coins) has a fickle taste. What is in great demand today may price itself out of the collector's pocketbook tomorrow. The neglected coin series of the present may have a spectacular future.

One area appears fairly safe for continued price rises— the very early coins of the United States. Those dated from about 1807 back to the start of U. S. Mint production in 1794 are almost certain to increase in value. The reason is quite obvious; there simply aren't enough to go around. For in those days, the annual mint output was reported in thousands, not millions or even billions, as today. And the number that survived over 150-odd years is even smaller.

Most persons are likely to consider that coins are not nearly as good an investment as common stocks. Possibly so. If you're interested solely in making money, there are undoubtedly other ways of making it faster, as well as losing it faster.

Of course, there's the reliably reported story of a man and his wife, each with $10,000 in cash to invest some 5 years ago. She was given the money by her husband to invest in the stock market. He put his $10,000 into coins. Not long ago, they compared gains. Her investment was nearly double the original $10,000; his had more than tripled in those 5 years.

It's interesting to compare coin prices over a 15-year period. Some will show spectacular rises, others will have had an increase of only 50 per cent or so, but almost all will at least have held their own.

If you could just be sure you'd be able to sell your coins for as much or a little more than you paid for them, you'd not have to worry about how much money you spent on your hobby. There are pitfalls, it is true, but as a person's knowledge of coins and their value increases, he's better able to follow old Ben Franklin's advice: "Don't pay too much for your whistle."

Let's take a look at some rarities in the United States coin world and see how they've fared. The 1799 large cent, in Fine condition, was quoted for $100 just 15 years ago. Now you'd have to pay more than $400 for the same coin.

The 1794 half dime, the first one issued by the U. S. Mint, was quoted at $30 in Fine condition; today the catalog value is close to $180. But the half dime of just one year later, 1795, a far commoner coin in terms of the number minted, shows a much more spectacular jump in value. From a quotation of $7.50 in Fine condition, the current price is around $125—an increase in value of more than 1,600 per cent.

You may wonder why the value of the coin of the earlier date increased only about 6 times, while the commoner half dime jumped more than 16 times. The answer is not too difficult. The type collector, eager to round out his collection of examples of half dime types, is quite content to buy the less expensive example of that first type.

Then the old economic law of supply-and-demand goes into action. An increased number of type collectors and a greater demand for the less expensive example of the 1794–1795 half dime sends the price up faster.

Some examples of the 15-year price rises in Rarities in *Fine* condition:

| The Coin | Date | Then | Now |
|---|---|---|---|
| One Cent | 1799 | $100.00 | $ 475.00 |
| Half Dime | 1794 | 30.00 | 175.00 |
| Half Dime | 1795 | 7.50 | 125.00 |
| Dime | 1796 (1st year) | 35.00 | 325.00 |
| Quarter | 1796 (1st year) | 60.00 | 1,700.00 |
| Half Dollar | 1794 (1st year) | 40.00 | 300.00 |
| Half Dollar | 1796 | 225.00 | 1,650.00 |
| Dollar | 1794 (1st year) | 300.00 | 2,000.00 |
| Dollar | 1795 | 20.00 | 125.00 |

Now let's look at some Scarcities (rather than Rarities) —all relatively modern coins, in *Uncirculated* condition:

| The Coin | Date | Then | Now |
|---|---|---|---|
| One Cent | 1909-S V D B | $ 12.50 | $ 165.00 |
| One Cent | 1914-D | 8.50 | 410.00 |
| Dime | 1916-D | 60.00 | 400.00 |
| Quarter | 1916 (Standing Liberty) | 65.00 | 500.00 |
| Quarter | 1918/7-S | 150.00 | 1,500.00 |

Silver dollars after 1878, with one notable exception, almost all show a decrease in value. The exception is the 1895 silver dollar of the Philadelphia mint in Proof condition. It has zoomed spectacularly from a value of $20 to $1,500 in about 15 years.

The 1878 silver dollar was cataloged at $5 in those days; now it's quoted at $3. A 1923 dollar, worth $10 then, is rated a $2.50 coin in Uncirculated condition today.

Silver dollars from 1794 to 1804 are quite valuable in almost all conditions. The Seated Liberty design, issued when dollar coinage was resumed in 1840, also has considerable

premium in the better conditions. But, starting with the
Morgan dollars in 1878, the best advice presently available
is: spend 'em.

Collectors generally fight shy of the later dollars—and
for a good and sufficient reason: there's no way of knowing
how many of a supposedly scarce date will suddenly glut
the market. In Federal Reserve Banks across the country are
stored unknown thousands of bright and shiny silver dollars,
all done up nicely in regulation canvas bags.

Each Christmas, or possibly for some other special occasion, some manufacturer or merchant or banker may decide to do the unusual—pay the employees or hand out
bonuses in the form of bright silver dollars. He applies to
his bank, the bank doesn't have enough on hand but can
get them from the nearest Federal Reserve Bank, and the
bags full of silver dollars are brought out of hiding. Over-
night, a dollar of a date that was supposedly scarce may
appear in quantity, and the value goes down to just what
it says on the coin—One Dollar.

So, for the most part, collectors are unwilling to pay premium prices for coins that are bulky, difficult to handle
and house properly, and may suddenly lose all or most of
their premium value.

However, the silver dollar series after 1878 may some day
experience a great boom. There are a few dealers and some
collectors betting on it.

CHAPTER FIVE

# The Value That
# Rubs Off

# THE VALUE THAT RUBS OFF

Value can go up—and value also can rub off. Let's visit a hypothetical coin shop and do a little eavesdropping.

The white-haired old lady came into the shop. Her manner was timid, almost apologetic.

"Are old coins—really old coins—worth anything?" she asked the man behind the counter.

"That all depends, madam."

"Well, when a coin is so old you can't even be sure about the date——" she began.

"Then 99 times out of a hundred it's just about worthless."

"Oh, dear—worthless?"

"It's always worth face value, of course. But a collector won't pay a premium for it. That's what I mean by worthless."

"I see." She paused. "Then—then—then that old dollar my grandfather left me isn't any good?"

The dealer was polite.

"I really don't know. Do you have it with you?" She nodded. "May I see it?"

She opened her handbag, fumbled through it, then pulled out an old yellow envelope. Carefully she took out a folded paper and unwrapped a large silver dollar. She handed it to the dealer. He studied it for a few moments, then:

"How much are you asking for it?"

The old lady brightened.

"You mean . . . it's . . . it's worth something? It's not too worn out?"

The dealer nodded.

"Well, I don't rightly know," she said. "You see, it belonged to my grandfather. He said his father gave it to him when it was brand new—that was—oh, maybe a hundred and fifty years ago. Grandfather carried it in his pocket for years—called it his good-luck dollar."

The dealer interrupted gently:

"And, by carrying it in his pocket, he wore off almost all its value."

The old lady was puzzled.

"I . . . I don't understand."

"This is a 1794 silver dollar, the first issued by the United States Mint. You can just make out the date. Brand new, this would be worth several thousand dollars. Not now.

"Your grandfather carried it too long as a good-luck piece. In this condition—so worn it couldn't be called better than About Good—well, it's not much more than a space filler."

"But you do think it's worth more than . . . just a dollar?"

There was a pathetic eagerness in the old lady's manner.

"Yes, it's worth more than just a dollar. How much are you asking for it?"

"Oh, dear, I don't really know." She paused, then asked timidly: "Would five dollars be too much?"

The dealer waited, then said: "You want five times face value?"

"Well, if that's too much——" she began.

"Not that—it's too little. I'll offer you one hundred dollars for this coin."

Her eyes widened.

"But even I can see that it isn't in very good condition." The dealer nodded. "Did you say . . . one hundred dollars?" He nodded again. "Well, I never! I ask if five dollars would be too much and you offer me a hundred. Are all you coin dealers this nice?"

"I'd like to think so, ma'am. Of course, as in every business, there are some rather sharp characters, and they don't care who they take advantage of——"

"Even white-haired old ladies?"

The dealer smiled.

"Sometimes especially white-haired old ladies."

There was a faint frown on the old lady's face.

"You'll be able to sell the dollar? You will get your money out of it?"

"Yes, ma'am—very definitely. I have a customer who specializes in collecting early silver dollars. He's been looking for a 1794 dollar for some time. Of course, he'd rather have one in better condition, but I'm fairly sure he'll buy this one—as a space filler—until a better one comes along."

So the dealer bought the About Good 1794 dollar, and everyone was happy. Even today, however, the dear old lady sometimes wishes her grandfather hadn't worn off so much of that dollar's value carrying it around in his pocket.

Admittedly, this scene is far from typical. There aren't many dealers who will volunteer a liberal offer to buy a coin. And in most shops, white-haired old ladies have long been considered fair game for sharpshooting.

Every coin, once it leaves the mint, starts to show signs of wear. In the normal course of circulation it goes through the entire scale until it reaches finally the condition known as Poor. The sooner it is rescued from continued circulation, the better its chances to survive as an acceptable collector's coin.

But a coin which has spent its years as a "pocket piece" shows unmistakable evidence of that fact. The rim, instead of being worn down gradually until the "reeding" (or so-called milling) fades and is gone, acquires a peculiar rounded appearance. This probably is caused by the fact that a pocket piece is usually carried in a pocket separate from the spending money. Its weight, as it jostles against the fabric of the pocket, wears down both sides of the edge until it appears almost rounded.

One such specimen encountered was a Lafayette commemorative dollar, a silver coin issued in 1900. The first United States coin authorized to bear the portrait of an American president—George Washington—the Lafayette dollar was sold by the Lafayette Memorial Commission for $2.

Such a dollar now has a catalog value of close to $75, if in Uncirculated condition. But the particular specimen which served some half a century as a pocket piece had a retail value a few years ago of exactly $5, which meant that the original owner spent about a dollar a year for the privilege of carrying it as a pocket piece.

But a dollar a year is cheap compared to the price paid by the person who used a $4 gold "Stella" as a pocket piece. The current price of a Stella (a short-lived experiment in an unusual denomination) is between $5,000 and $13,000, depending on whether it was issued in 1879 or 1880 and whether the particular specimen is of the Barber design (a total of 430 struck in both years) or the Morgan design (only 20 struck in the two years).

This particular Stella, which may have served as a pocket piece for as long as 80 years, when finally rescued from oblivion, was so worn that only the distinctive 5-pointed star could be made out. The date was gone and it was impossible to tell whether it was Barber or Morgan design.

With an effort, one could make out that there once had been a portrait on the obverse side, but whether it was the less scarce 1879 with flowing hair, or the extremely valuable 1880 with coiled hair, was lost forever. Even the gold weight was far below what it should have been—all due to wear in some man's pocket.

What was its value? Although in original Proof condition it would be worth thousands of dollars today, a dealer had difficulty finding someone willing to pay $25 for it! At that rate of depreciation, the cost of carrying that pocket piece was somewhere between $55 and $112 a year.

There are many coins which have proved popular as pocket pieces: the Columbian half dollars, the Stone Mountain Memorial halves and the Washington-Carver issues. That such coins lead a happy-go-lucky life in the depths of a man's pocket is of no particular concern. They were issued in such quantities that the irrevocable loss of many such specimens is a mere drop in the numismatic bucket.

Early coins sometimes have value literally bounced off. The early United States silver dollars were large and quite heavy. If dropped onto a hard surface from a considerable height, edge dents or "bumps" appear. While these may not deflate a good coin's market value greatly, they will tend to make the coin "less desirable," and consequently it will not command as high a price as the same coin in similar condition free of such edge bumps.

For years, a coin with a hole was looked upon with disfavor by U.S. collectors. As recently as 10 years ago, dealers sometimes had difficulty selling them for 10 per cent of their catalog value.

No one knows for certain why many of the earlier coins of the United States were holed. They couldn't all be worn as charms on a necklace or bracelet. Some *may* have been used as makeshift teething rings; a holed dollar of the 1790s was found with what appear to be nicks such as might have been left as a result of use by many teething babies.

Holing of dollars and quarters and halves and large cents appears to have been fairly widespread as late as 1876. One collector has found a quarter, a half dollar and a trade dollar of that year, 1876, each with a neat hole at the top of the obverse. And all were in nearly Extremely Fine condition. Could these holes have been drilled recently? It hardly appears likely, since the catalog value of the three is close to $50, and not many persons tamper with that much value, even for the girl friend's bangle bracelet.

This is not to say that drilling holes in coins stopped abruptly in 1876; late-date Indian cents, a Buffalo nickel and a Walking Liberty half dollar have been encountered so holed.

Do holed coins have a future? It would appear that the early United States specimens have a very bright future. Whereas the 10 per cent of catalog was the old rule of thumb, many dealers today are asking—and getting—as much as 100 per cent of catalog value.

In Europe today, an ancient Roman or Greek coin with a hole is often displayed alongside those which are completely sound. And the price asked is exactly the same—with hole or without.

Early American coins with holes have had a steady increase in value because there simply aren't enough fine, sound coins to go around. When collectors of United States coins could be counted in the hundreds or low thousands, there were enough coins for all. Today, although the exact figure is anybody's guess, the number of serious coin collectors in this country is estimated to be well into the hundreds of thousands.

While it might be a wonderful state of affairs if every collector who wanted a prime specimen of, say, a 1795 half dollar could get it, it just can't be done today. So the early half with a hole is being looked upon with more and more favor.

In 1800, the United States Mint reported that it turned out 11,622 Half Eagles—$5 gold pieces. How many have survived is not known. Its catalog value today ranges from $175 in Fine condition to $375 in Uncirculated.

How much would such a coin, in Extremely Fine condition but with a small neat hole in it, be worth? Under the old schedule, it would be valued at about $25. But don't be surprised that that early gold piece, even with a hole, is valued by its present owner at more than $150. And he doesn't want to sell it.

The moral of all this is:

1. Don't carry a potentially valuable coin as a pocket piece.

2. Avoid dropping that 1797 silver dollar on the tile floor.

3. Holes in classic American coins aren't as damaging as they used to be.

CHAPTER SIX

# What Makes
# a Coin Collector?

# WHAT MAKES A COIN COLLECTOR?

Answer to the question "What makes a coin collector?" is by no means simple. Almost without exception, the real collector became interested in coins quite by accident. He didn't just sit down one day and say to himself, "I shall become a numismatist." Chances are he couldn't even spell the word, much less define it.

Probably most were earlier collectors of something or other: match covers, cigar bands, hotel towels. Many are graduates of (or refugees from) philately—the collecting of stamps. One such former philatelist, who doesn't care whose toes he tramps on, explains why he left stamps:

"The modern stamp is about as exciting as a picture postcard. It doesn't really represent any value—merely the promise of some government to deliver a letter or postcard someplace or other.

"Sure, they're colorful, sometimes even well designed. But too many are put out by foreign governments for the sucker trade—the U.S. stamp collector who *must* have the latest issue of this or that newly-formed nation.

"More than one small principality derives most if not all its expenses of government from the sale of such stamps to U.S. collectors. I don't mind being played for a sucker occasionally, but, as a steady diet, I revolt.

"Then, stamps are such fragile things. An insect may chew one into a lacy network of nothing. Damaged perforations can ruin the value of a stamp. An unfortunate cancellation may obscure the design and make that particular example almost worthless.

"But when I really lost interest in stamp collecting was the day I discovered that, on a brand new stamp, the lack of OG (that translates to 'original gum') could cut the value in half. Anything so ephemeral a determinant of value as the glue on a stamp's backside was just too much. I gave up my stamp collection, started seriously on coins, and have never regretted the switch.

"For, while an excess of humidity in the air may cause a silver coin to take on a certain amount of discoloration, it has never yet caused it to lose half its value. And I've never lost a coin to any insect, no matter how hungry it may have been."

One man became a serious collector of Chinese coins quite by accident. A number of years ago, while digging in China, he unearthed some early Chinese cash. The coins, while they meant little to him at first glance, soon fascinated him. He decided to learn more about them and, as his knowledge of them and their history increased, he soon found himself a serious collector and before much longer something of an authority.

Another, before he became a serious collector, was stranded in a small southern town over a long Fourth of July week end. On the Saturday before that long week end started, he wandered through the somewhat limited business district.

He glanced idly in the window of a stamp and coin shop. Displayed were a few examples of the early bust-type half dollar—the ones which have lettering around the edge reading "Fifty Cents or Half a Dollar." For some years he had had a mild interest in this particular type of coin, but had never before had the time or opportunity to learn much about them.

He went into the store, bought 10 or 12 of those early halves at modest prices, and asked to buy or borrow some books on the subject of United States coins. In the ensuing long week end, his mild interest developed into a serious hobby. His specialty today is still the early halves—from 1794 through 1836—although his collection has become somewhat diversified over the years.

An Army sergeant, who had collected stamps in his youth, was stationed in North Africa during World War II. Somewhere he got possession of a coin of the Roman Empire. As he recalls it, it was one issued by Constantine the Great—not a particularly valuable coin, by any means—but it was sufficient to interest him in ancient coins.

Later he was stationed in Italy and spent some time in Greece. He located and bought more and more coins of the ancient world. When he was returned to the United States on rotation, the coins he brought back were found to weigh some 43 pounds. Fortunately, the return trip was made by ocean vessel.

On return to civilian life, he checked over his accumulation and decided to dispose of duplicates and those in poorer condition. The remainder formed the nucleus of what today is a fine collection of coins of the Emperor Hadrian, who ruled Rome from A.D. 117 to 138. The different coins of this particular Roman Emperor number in the thousands, and the sergeant admits his collection may never be entirely complete.

More than one person has become a collector because a relative gave him a few unfamiliar American coins. After all, the youngster of today may know a lot about rockets and outer space, but does he know that his forefathers spent half cents and 3-cent pieces and half dimes, and that the large cent of more than a hundred years ago always contained a full cent's worth of copper? Curiosity and desire to know more about such early American coins have led many a youngster into the serious business of coin collecting.

One thing which did much to encourage the collecting of United States coins by series and dates was the development of coin folders. Here was a booklike set of cardboard pages with holes cut, into which could be fitted the proper Lincoln cents or Buffalo nickels or Standing Liberty quarters.

Parents saw in such coin folders an opportunity to give Junior a hobby and possibly develop in him an interest in saving money instead of spending every cent. Most of the holes could be filled from pocket change.

But, as most fathers later found out, in every set of United States coins there are stumbling blocks—the "key dates." These are coins which, because they were minted in small quantities and not put aside in bulk, today command considerable premiums. When Junior wants that missing Lincoln cent to complete his collection, Pop goes to a coin dealer. He's in a generous mood, willing to pay as much as a dollar—maybe even $2—to get that coin and make Junior happy.

Then he learns that he'll have to lay out $50 or more to buy a passable example of that particular key date.

And at this point, Pop can be excused for wondering if he was so wise in buying Junior that inexpensive little coin folder.

It has been estimated that probably 95 per cent of all Americans have a cache of coins. It often is not more than a few coins which, because they're bright and shiny, or because they "look different," or because they are old, are put aside. Some are tossed in a corner of a drawer, others are kept in an old cigar box, still others are carefully put into some sort of a bag.

Now, these persons are not coin collectors in any sense of the word. Depending on the size of the cache, they might be called coin accumulators or simply coin savers.

Nearly all collectors started out as accumulators. It was

only as their knowledge of coins increased, and certain likes and dislikes developed, that they left the accumulator group and joined the ranks of collectors.

Will every accumulator become a collector? By no means! To some, a coin represents simply a unit of purchasing power and nothing more. It may be a beautiful dime, well struck and almost uncirculated. So what? It's good to buy the evening newspaper.

Which accumulators will become collectors? Only time or an accident will tell.

# CHAPTER SEVEN

## *What to Collect*

# WHAT TO COLLECT

If you should decide to become a coin collector, the first question that may puzzle you is: "What should I collect?" Fortunately, there is no single answer.

Some collectors may specialize in the coins of ancient Greece. Others stick to the Roman Republic or the Roman Empire. Some collect foreign coins. Still others seek coins of as many different foreign countries as possible.

Most Americans decide to collect United States coins. Since these are the coins a person encounters every day, the choice is easily understandable.

The first choice of any youngster is, quite naturally, the current Lincoln head cents. Two folders, complete with holes into which the cents can be inserted, are available for less than a dollar.

Theoretically, Lincoln cents of every date and every mint are still in circulation. But—and it's a large "but"— certain of them are almost impossible to find. Too many persons have been on the lookout for them too long for them to be located easily in change. They are the so-called key dates, and the list includes the 1909-S with the designer's initials, "V D B," on the reverse, the 1909-S without the initials, the 1914-D and the 1931-S.

Certain collectors periodically go to their local banks and purchase rolls of cents, which they painstakingly search for the valuable key dates. Occasionally they are rewarded. However, unless one is very young, has excellent eyesight and lots of time on his hands, this procedure is not recommended.

If the roll-searcher ever stopped to figure out the hourly cost of such all-too-frequently fruitless searches, he'd be aghast. He's working at worse than coolie wages. If he could compute the eyestrain resulting from searching through thousands of Lincoln cents, he'd soon decide there are better uses to which his eyes could be put. But, as previously noted, for the very young with time on their hands, it's one way of trying to complete a Lincoln cent collection.

Other beginners may start with the Jefferson nickels or even the so-called Buffalo nickels. The latter are increasingly difficult to find in the earlier dates, although Jefferson nickels of almost every date and mint can be encountered in change. A key Jefferson is the 1950-D which can be located in circulation only very occasionally; most of them appear to have been put away in Uncirculated rolls. So the day may be coming when a 1950 Jefferson nickel of the Denver mint which shows some signs of actual circulation may be worth more than an Uncirculated example.

In the quarter division, the Washington 25-cent piece is in current circulation and almost all dates and mints can be located fairly easily. There are some stoppers—such as the 1932 and 1936 of the Denver and San Francisco branch mints—but even they occasionally can be found in pocket change (well worn, of course).

Half dollars of the current Ben Franklin series have not had much favor as yet. In absolutely Uncirculated condition and sharply struck, they are attractive. But that attractiveness disappears to a large extent after only brief circulation.

The earlier half dollars—the Walking Liberty type, minted from 1916 through 1947—are still circulating freely, and a set can be put together almost entirely from circulation. Even the key dates of 1921 and 1921-D can be purchased in Good condition at a still-reasonable figure.

Maybe you don't know what you'd like to collect. In that event, spend your time just accumulating—cents, nickels, dimes and quarters. After getting together an accumulation of this type, look it over some day. Arrange like coins in rows and by dates. Study them. Possibly one series appeals to you more than the others. If so, you've found the denomination or denominations in which you may want to specialize.

Suppose the series is the Washington quarters. You concentrate on getting together as many dates as you can, in the best possible condition. In the course of examining your pocket change, you may encounter a Standing Liberty quarter (1916 through 1930). Perhaps the design interests you, and you will decide to collect this earlier series. Then you run onto a somewhat worn Barber quarter of the 1892–1916 era and, somewhat hesitantly, you add this series to your specialty. And so on back to the very beginning—the 1796 quarter, the very first 25-cent piece issued by the United States Mint.

But maybe you don't want to start collecting out of current change. Perhaps you find a certain early series to be most attractive and decide to collect that from the very start. In that event, of course, you'll have to buy or trade or have given to you every coin in your collection, because such coins simply aren't to be found in circulation today.

Certain early series haven't yet caught on seriously with the coin-collecting fraternity, and the prices for specimens in excellent condition from these series are relatively low.

For example, half dimes of the period from 1829 through 1873 are not too difficult to acquire at reasonable prices. Of course, if, after having completed the 1829–1873 series, you decide to go back to 1794 through 1805, you're in for some expensive trouble, for coins in merely Good condition in this period start at $50 each and go as high as $900 in Uncirculated.

Some collectors, when they start to specialize, are not happy until they have acquired every single date of that series. If one has unlimited funds with which to purchase coins, it's quite all right to have that attitude. But there are hundreds who specialize in various series and have occasional gaps. Perhaps they'd be happier if they could fill those gaps without too-great strain, but they decline to mortgage the old homestead. Instead, they learn to live with those blank spaces.

Another series which has been neglected for many years is the half cent, the smallest United States denomination. First issued in 1793, the coin continued in use (although not continuously minted) through 1857.

Because they have not had the popularity of, for example, the early large copper cents, the more common dates are still reasonably priced. But there are certain dates in this thus-far neglected series which command high prices. So the half-cent collector must not be too unhappy if there are some blank spaces in his collection. (Unless, of course, he is equipped with the proverbial "money to burn," in which case he needn't have started on a neglected series in the first place.)

The bust-type half dollars, dating from 1807 through 1836, were scorned by collectors for many years. They were relatively common even in Fine or better condition, because they saw very little actual circulation. With the disappearance of the United States silver dollar during the period from 1804 to 1840, those half dollars were the largest silver coin available for exchange purposes. These bust-type halves would be put into bags at one bank and transferred intact to another bank. Seldom did they reach actual person-to-person circulation; they spent most of their lives in the darkness of canvas bags.

When the United States finally resumed coinage of silver

dollars in 1840, the bust half dollars were released from their roles of interbank medium of exchange. By that time, however, a new type of half dollar was in use and those which went into circulation were before long put away by their owners as "different" (and possibly valuable) half dollars.

Mint records show that these early halves were never issued in unusually large quantities. The smallest coinage was in 1815, with a total of 47,150; in 1820 the next smallest coinage was 751,122. The highest yearly mintage of this early bust-type half was in 1834—fewer than 6½ million.

While these bust halves were the poor cousins of the numismatic world for many years, recently they have started to come into their own. In recent years, it has become increasingly difficult to locate Uncirculated examples, and prices have gone up accordingly. But specimens in Fine condition still can be purchased at relatively low prices.

The bust-type half is a series which contains no less than 17 distinct "overdates," wherein a die from a previous year was used for the current year, the new year numeral having been punched over that of the preceding year. Such overdates exist in almost all of the early coin series and usually command a special premium among collectors.

Repunching last year's die to bring it up to date was an essential labor-saving device in the days when each die of any United States coin was practically handmade. In the early days, mass production of working dies from a master die was unknown. When new dies were needed, workmen had to punch into the blank the various symbols which were to appear on the finished coin.

Using the bust-type half as an example, the workman first may have punched in the bust of Liberty. Then he punched in the 13 stars around the obverse. Finally he punched in the current date. These various punches, even though apparently alike, differed widely: one numeral "2," for example, might have a curled base, another a straight base, and so on.

It was impossible for the early workman to punch those stars in exactly the some positions relative to the bust. On the reverse, punches for the letters in "United States of America" varied frequently, some being without a single flaw, others having a serif or two missing, still others being bifurcated.

So those early half dollars might be said to be as close to handmade as any coins ever minted by the United States.

Today, the novice coin collector may be conned into paying a fancy price for a "small date" 1960 Lincoln cent. He's buying a "rarity" that isn't rare—only a minor deviation in a die from which millions of such small-date cents were struck.

Die variations—real and unmistakable and that can be seen with the naked eye—abound in the early United States coins and, if you specialize, they're really worth collecting. The specialist in early United States coinage often pays a good premium for a special die variety which may be lacking in his particular collection.

So there can be said to be at least 3 answers to the problem as to what to collect.

1. Collect the obvious. Buy a coin folder and select your nickels or dimes or cents from those you get in change every day.

2. Accumulate until you can decide. Try several different series (get them as close to Uncirculated as possible). Before long you'll find one or more that really appeals to you.

3. Read about coins and study as much as you can, then

specialize from the start. This is the more expensive way to collect coins, but it's generally agreed to be the most satisfying and (if you're at all interested) rewarding in a monetary way.

CHAPTER EIGHT

## *There Are Such Things as Phonies*

# THERE *ARE* SUCH THINGS AS PHONIES

As in all areas of antiques (and coins can be classified as antiques whether they're 100-year-old American examples or those of Ancient Rome), there are dishonest individuals out to make a few fast bucks from the unwary and the uninitiated.

Naturally, those coins which have the greatest market value are selected for doctoring or faking in some way or another. Ancient gold has been copied with varying degrees of success for hundreds of years. Even ancient and medieval silver has been reproduced almost too well. But who'd think there are those who'd doctor an American cent to look like what it isn't?

In the field of United States coins, there are three principal means which occasionally are used to make collectors' items.

First is the restrike, a sometimes legitimate production of the U. S. Mint, but not legitimately produced in the purported year of issue. Through the unofficial efforts of certain mint workers in the past, rare coins have been produced to meet the demand—and cash—of collectors.

Second is the doctored coin: the mint mark of a common dollar is removed to make it a rarity; part of a numeral is cut away to make it look like another; a Buffalo's leg is chiseled off to make it resemble the legitimate 3-legged rarity.

Third is the deliberate attempt to make the proverbial silk purse out of a sow's ear. In such an attempt, a character secretly copper-plates a steel cent of 1943 to make it appear as an accidental product (and hence a supposed rarity) of the official U. S. Mint. Sharpers sometimes buff silver coins to make them appear to be the mirror-finished proofs of a premium year. Such coins would never fool an expert numismatist, but they have been sold at "bargain" prices to the unwary.

Of course, the out-and-out counterfeit is not an attempt to fool the coin collectors, but to defraud the United States government. While counterfeiting is not practiced much in this country today, due to an alert Secret Service, there was the case of a man who issued his own Jefferson nickels in considerable quantity back in 1944.

His copies were good enough to go unnoticed for several years. Then an alert coin collector detected the almost minor oversight of the copyist. In that war year (1944), the United States nickel bore the mint mark "P" above the dome of Jefferson's Monticello home. The counterfeiter failed to include that small detail in his version of the 1944 Jefferson nickel, and it led to his undoing.

There are those who won't quarrel with the restrike, even though it admittedly was struck some time *after* the year of original issue. In the case of certain coin dates, restrikes are the only ones available. But, where an original and a restrike of a certain date can be had, the original coin almost always commands a higher premium.

One of the better-known restrikes is the 1804 large copper cent. This fake was manufactured in about 1860 by some employees of the U. S. Mint. The 1804 large cent has always been more or less of a rarity, and there undoubtedly was a considerable demand for it even a hundred years ago. But whether the mint workers fabricated the fake to make money or merely to please friends and relatives, is not known.

The 1804 restrike probably would never fool a numismatist worthy of the name. The workers found a discarded and rusty die of 1804, somewhat cracked and battered. They didn't bother to find (or couldn't locate) a reverse die of the proper type. Instead they settled for one of the style used some 14 years later.

The resulting restrike is a coin well-pitted on the obverse and with a reverse design that doesn't match those which preceded or immediately followed it. This so-called 1804 restrike, in Uncirculated condition, is valued at about a fourth as much as a genuine 1804 in only Fine condition.

The large silver dollar of that same year—1804—is probably the most publicized rarity of all American coins. Whenever it is offered for sale at auction, it is likely to bring in the neighborhood of $30,000.

There is a great big mystery as to what happened to the 19,570 silver dollars which the mint director reported were coined between January 7 and March 28, 1804. Coinage of silver dollars was stopped abruptly on that date by the mint to prevent exportation abroad, because its bullion value was greater than a dollar.

Were the 19,570 coined up to the March day tossed back into the melting pot? It would appear likely, but no one can be certain.

Through the years, various other theories as to the disappearance of those 1804 dollars have been advanced. They include:

The dollars were exported immediately, either as coin or as bullion.

They were put aboard a vessel bound for China, and the vessel and its cargo were lost at sea.

The entire production was exported to the Far East.

They were part of tribute paid to the Barbary pirates.

All were captured by the British.

The 19,000 were stolen and are presently buried—where, no one knows.

The 14 or so examples of the 1804 dollar in existence to-day are known as "originals" and "restrikes." It is possible that half of these, dubbed "originals," were the seven 1804 silver dollars reserved for assay. The "restrikes" probably were struck at the Philadelphia mint between 1836 and 1842, although no one can say for sure.

Phony 1804 dollars, outright fakes, have been fabricated: some so cleverly that they fool even the experts—for a time. The usual way to manufacture a phony 1804 is to secure an 1801 dollar, remove the final "1" in the date and solder a "4" onto the coin in its place.

Careful study with the strongest magnifying glass might reveal the alteration to an expert. To the average collector, only the "bargain" price asked might keep him from ac-quiring it—that and the knowledge that such fake 1804 dollars do exist.

The doctored coin is one that started life legitimately enough but somewhere along the way fell into the hands of a get-rich-quick artist and was transformed into an imita-tion of a much more valuable brother.

An excellent example of the coin which may be doctored is the 1944 Lincoln cent produced by the Denver mint. In all, more than 430 million such Lincolns were struck there. Its catalog value, even in the shiniest of Uncirculated, is less than 50 cents.

But little old 1944 has a rich ancestor—the 1914 Lincoln cent that also had its birthplace in Denver. This wealthy relative of 1914 is currently rated at well above $400 in Uncirculated.

Conniving souls on occasion have sought to level out this difference in financial rating. Through dextrous use of en-

# What You Can Do

1. They're still legal tender. That 3-cent nickel, with the Roman numeral III, may look unfamiliar to most Americans, but it's still a spendable coin worth every one of the 3 cents called for. You might have even more difficulty spending the 2-cent bronze coin of 1864—it just doesn't look like any other coin ever issued by the U. S. Mint.

1

2. Don't be fooled by age. One is older by 16 centuries, but it's cheaper. The coin of ancient Rome, issued during the rule of Alexander Severus, A.D. 222-235, is worth around $10 or so. But the United States cent is the much sought-after 1864 Indian Head with initial "L" of Engraver Longacre. In Uncirculated condition, it brings over $150.

2

3. They'll make someone happy. Foreign coins of this type have an actual collector's value of only a few cents apiece, even though some may be from lands halfway around the world. Regardless of actual worth, such coins can make a youngster happy, for they have real play value. That they represent hard cash to someone someplace is quite enough.

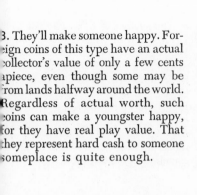

3

# Some U.S. Classics

4

4. The first of these two coins is a 1795 half cent, series started in 1793. It is one of 25,600 half cents which the mint reported it made during that year, and today is quoted around $90 in Very Fine. The second is the extremely valuable 1799 large cent —a "key coin" in this series. In Very Fine condition it is rated as worth over $600, yet the mint report says that 904,585 were struck in 1799.

5

5. The half dime of 1795 (second year of issue) has shown a remarkable rise in value in recent years. As a "type coin," it is much sought after by type collectors and its market price consequently has risen sharply. The dime is dated 1796—first year of issue, when some 22,135 were coined. In Uncirculated condition, it is rated close to $1,000.

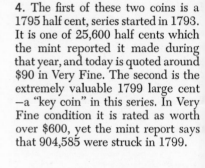

6

6. The smaller of these two coins is a Half Eagle or $5 gold piece, dated 1803. Liberty, as depicted here, looks more like a refugee from the French Revolution than an American figure. On the large silver dollar of 1802, Liberty has a ribbon in her hair and disdains to wear any sort of a cap. Because each had more value as metal than as a coin, few escaped somebody's melting pot.

# The Changes in a Coin

7. First coin is a superb specimen of the 1805 quarter dollar. Obverse design was the same as that of 1796, the first year of issue, and follows the pattern of early half dimes and dimes. The second quarter dollar shows Liberty wearing a cap that was reasonably fashionable in 1818 —at least on coins.

7

8. Americans had to get along with quarter dollars of reduced size from 1831 on. The 1834 coin shown here looks about the same as the second style—only it was smaller. Starting in 1838, Liberty had an opportunity to sit down and she kept that seat for some 53 years, glancing coyly over her right shoulder.

8

9. The quarter was reduced in weight in 1853 and the event was celebrated by arrows on each side of the date for 3 years. By 1892, Charles E. Barber decided Americans should have a good look at Liberty's face so he designed the dime, quarter, and half-dollar series which continued through 1916.

9

10. Liberty was given a chance to stand up in 1916. But the Standing Liberty quarter, a beautiful coin as it came from the mint, didn't stand up too well in circulation and was discontinued after 1930. The Washington quarter of 1932, originally designed as a sort of Commemorative coin, is still being minted.

10

# Just How Valuable?

11

11. Some collectors view a holed coin with undisguised disdain. Yet here is a 1795 large cent, well holed, that would give pause to the snootiest collector. The obverse looks like a somewhat well-worn specimen. But the reverse is enough to startle anyone. Design, date, and lettering are reversed—yet the image is cameo rather than intaglio. What happened? How? What's its value? How much is a unique coin worth?

12

12. This 1805 quarter dollar doesn't look too impressive. It's sufficiently worn to grade somewhere between Very Good and Fine—catalog somewhere between $50 and $75. Now look at the 1819 quarter. It's well worn and the catalog would place it somewhere under $20. But observe the date—die breaks have really made a mess of it. If you check the authority on early quarter dollars, A. W. Browning, you find that it is a No. 4—"a very rare variety." And to a quarter-dollar collector, it's worth a lot more than a mere $20 or so.

13

13. This $1 gold coin is not the best-struck gold dollar in the world; it shows definite wear and there are indications it may once have been soldered. Yet it is one of the most valuable in the entire series. It is an 1860-D gold dollar, of which exactly 1,566 were made at the small branch mint in Dahlonega, Georgia, just one year before the Civil War started. Its catalog is somewhere between $1,500 and $2,500—quite an increase for a mere dollar's worth of gold.

# These Made Coin Collectors

14. Early coins from an ancestor's trunk. A pair of coppers, such as these, started one person as a coin collector. A 1795 large cent, somewhat the worse for wear, and a Fugio cent of 1787, first coin to be issued by authority of the United States, were found in an attic storeroom and became the basis for a first-rate coin collection.

14

15. Ancients interest a World War II soldier. When on duty in North Africa in 1943, an American GI acquired a bronze coin from the reign of Constantine the Great (A.D. 306–337). Despite the fact that it was not particularly valuable, its age fascinated him. When later stationed in Italy, he added other ancient coins such as the silver tetradrachm of Athens (400–330 B.C.) and became a serious collector.

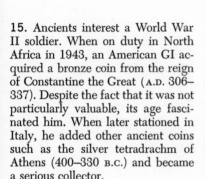

15

16. Casual interest into absorbing hobby. Bust-type half dollars, such as this 1822 example, displayed in a coin store window of a small southern town, caused one casually interested visitor to become a serious collector of the series (1807–1839). Such halves, once considered a drug on the market, have recently come into their own.

16

# Designs on Coins

17

17. These distinctive designs guaranteed the purity and weight of metal in early coins. An owl (490–430 B.C.) indicated that this coin was issued by Athens which guaranteed it, while a rose was the official city mark of Rhodus on the Island of Rhodes (400-333 B.C.).

18

18. Pegasus, the flying horse of mythology, was featured on the coins of Corinth (337–300 B.C.). The tetradrachm from the reign of Alexander the Great of Macedon (336–323 B.C.) is supposed to show Hercules, wearing a lion skin. But everyone claims Alexander posed for the portrait. That's Zeus seated on the reverse.

19

19. "Liberty herself appears to be in a fright." The large cent of 1793 met with considerable criticism from the public. Even the reverse met objections—"The chain...is but a bad omen for Liberty." The redesigned large cent of 1794 shows Liberty considerably calmed.

**20.** Real Indian or white girl? The so-called Indian cent (1859–1909) may or may not show a real Indian. There's a legend that Engraver Longacre's young daughter was visiting the mint one day when an Indian chief put his war bonnet on her head. The effect was said to be so striking that Longacre made a quick sketch of his daughter and later used it in designing the coin.

**21.** Unchanged for 50 years. The Lincoln cent holds the record for longevity (50-odd years) although a change in the reverse was made in 1959. In that year, the long familiar wheat ears were replaced by a picture of the Lincoln Memorial.

**22.** The sharper's delight. The 5-cent nickel of 1883 first appeared without the word "Cents" on it. Dishonest characters are said to have gold-plated such nickels and passed them off in rural areas as 5-dollar gold pieces. The word "Cents" was put in place of "E Pluribus Unum" later in 1883.

**23.** This was Black Diamond. There is no doubt as to the identity of the bison on the so-called Buffalo nickel (1913–1938)—it was Black Diamond, one-time resident of the New York Zoological Gardens. As for the Indian, although many claimed sole honor, the designer actually used 3 different models.

**24.** Abruptly Liberty became more modest. When the Standing Liberty quarter was first issued (1916) only 52,000 were minted. Next year more than 12 million were issued—and somebody appears to have been shocked by Liberty's attire, because later that year the quarter was redesigned. In this second variety, Liberty wears a full coat of mail—much more modest. The Standing Liberty quarter was relatively short-lived, being discontinued after 1930.

20    21

22    23

24

# Recognize These Coins?

25

25. This Columbian Exposition half dollar (1892) should be familiar to many Americans—it is one of the commonest of all Commemorative coins. More than two and a half million were coined in 1892 and 1893. They were designed to sell for $1 each. But at the close of the exposition, many were left unsold. They were later released for circulation at face value.

26

26. The Isabella quarter dollar issued in 1893 also at the Columbian Exposition, is far less familiar. Only 24,124 were minted. They also were sold for $1 each but none was deliberately put into circulation. The price today for an Uncirculated example is well above the $60 mark. The foreign monarch pictured is Queen Isabella of Spain.

27

27. George Washington finally made the grade on this Commemorative dollar. The Lafayette dollar (1900) was the first coin authorized by the United States to carry the portrait of a president. On the coin's reverse appears the equestrian statue of General Lafayette in Paris, gift of the American people. Total coinage was 36,026.

# A Mint Is Started

**28.** From Martha's silverware? This is a half disme, first product of the newly established U. S. Mint, dated 1792. It is said that George Washington took some of the family silverware to the new mint so that some small silver coins could be struck. Portrait on the coin is said to be that of Martha Washington.

28

**29.** You were expected to know their value. Early gold and silver coins of the United States failed to carry any indication of value on either side. One was expected to know that the smaller coin was a half dime, the other a full dime.

29

**30.** Early Eagles were sometimes skinny. The $5 gold piece of 1795 depicted a somewhat scrawny eagle on its reverse, while the 1806 quarter dollar's heraldic eagle was larger but still not too healthy in appearance.

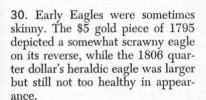

30

**31.** Portrait of Peter, the mint eagle. Christian Gobrecht designed this pattern dollar in 1836. On the reverse, he put a portrait of the famed Philadelphia mint eagle, Peter, in full flight. Peter's portrait also is carried on the Flying Eagle cents of 1856 through 1858.

31

# Three Classifications

**32.** *Impossible* to find in circulation. These first 3 types of U.S. half dollars simply aren't in circulation any more. If you tried to spend one, you might have some difficulty since the public no longer is familiar with the designs on them. Started in 1794, these designs were typical through 1839.

**33.** These halves are *Unlikely* in your change. The Seated Liberty half dollars have almost vanished from circulation, while the Barber halves, when found in change, are usually so worn as to have almost no premium value. The 1854 half dollar had arrows at the date to indicate a decrease in weight.

**34.** *Possible* to find circulating freely. The Walking Liberty half dollar (reverse with pantalooned eagle shown here) is frequently encountered in a person's daily change, although the earlier dates may be almost worn out. The Franklin half dollar (both sides shown here), appearing first in 1948, has only a few dates with premium value unless absolutely Uncirculated.

# Unfamiliar U.S. Coins

**35.** The half cent, dated 1850, would come in handy in these days of sales taxes. Larger than today's 1-cent piece, it contained a full half cent's worth of copper. Unfortunately, in 1858 it joined the dodo bird in oblivion. The large cent of 1832 would cause consternation if it suddenly appeared in pocket change today.

35

**36.** A 2-cent piece, such as the 1864 example shown here, would have little excuse for existence today—it would buy practically nothing, not even a newspaper, and it wouldn't fit modern slot machines. This short-lived coin was notable for being the first to carry the motto "In God We Trust."

36

**37.** The 3-cent pieces, whether nickel or silver, would find little acceptance now. The 3-cent silver shown here is dated 1855—one of the more valuable in the series, its present price Uncirculated being well over $75. The 3-cent nickel was last minted in 1889.

37

**38.** The 20-cent piece lasted only 4 years—1875 through 1878. The public generally disliked the coin—it was too similar in size and design to the quarter dollar. If one looked closely, he could see that the eagle on the reverse differed from the quarter dollar bird and that the edge was plain. But at a casual glance, there was confusion.

38

# Unusual U.S. Coins

39

40          41

**39. Easy to lose dollars.** The 3 types of gold dollars shown here were small enough to get lost in and from the average pocket or purse. First type (1849–1854) was the smallest coin ever minted by the United States. Second size (1854-1856) was larger in diameter but thinner. On Type 3 (1856–1889), Liberty was given a different and larger head.

**40. The high-priced lady.** This is Stella, the $4 gold pattern coin of 1879 and 1880. Illustrated is the least expensive of the series—the Flowing Hair type, dated 1879, selling today in the neighborhood of $6,000 in Proof state. From this modest figure, the others range up to between $11,000 and $13,500.

**41. The "poor relation."** For the collector who couldn't afford a $4 gold piece, there was the $3 gold—also an unusual denomination. Until a few years ago, an example could be acquired for around $40 in Uncirculated condition. Today, the least expensive starts around $200. Never popular, these coins saw little actual circulation.

**42. Dollars for the Orient.** To compete with Mexican silver circulating in the Orient, the U.S. minted trade dollars from 1873 through 1885. Legal tender in amounts up to $5 at the start, trade dollars later were restricted to export use only. Uncirculated, they are valued from as little as $13 to as high as $250. Certain Proofs are quoted at $6,000 to $9,000.

42

graving tools, they doctor the first "4" of the 1944 cent, and before long it straightens out to look very much like the "1" in the rich relative of 1914.

Such altered-date coins have been offered in the past; they will be in the future. One quick check can be made: the doctored 1944 has too much space between the "9" and the "1," where everything but the upright of the "4" has been removed.

Proof positive can be found through use of a good magnifying glass. The designer's initials "V D B" can be seen on Lincoln's right shoulder, near the rim, on the altered 1944-D. Genuine 1914-D Lincoln cents did not carry these initials. Sharpers sometimes even try to tool away the tiny initials from the 1944 coin, but a good glass will reveal the scratches made in the effort.

Less common, but by no means rare, is the "doctored" 1909-S Indian cent. Here the relatively common 1909 Indian is made into his rarer brother from the San Francisco mint. How? By soldering a tiny "S" to the correct spot on the reverse side. Some sharpers do not even bother to use solder, being fairly confident that ordinary glue will hold the "S" in place until they can depart to safer climes.

An 1895 silver dollar of the Philadelphia mint (no mint mark) is cataloged at well over a thousand dollars in Proof condition. It is a challenge that would appeal to any good con man. So he may take an Uncirculated 1895 dollar minted at New Orleans (catalog value around $60) and carefully remove the "O" mint letter.

The result is an 1895 dollar that would easily fool the average collector. It looks exactly like the thousand-dollar Philadelphia job, except that a powerful magnifying glass will show minute scratches in the area from which the unwanted mint letter was removed.

Less valuable, but still worth a dishonest effort by the confidence clan, is the 3-legged Buffalo nickel produced at the Denver mint in 1937. The genuine coin shows the Buffalo with only three legs, the fourth having almost disappeared as a result of a break in the die.

The sharper takes a regular 1937-D nickel and carefully tools away the offending fourth leg. The result is that a coin cataloging only $3.50 now looks like a rarity with a $90 catalog value.

So, unless you can spot a doctored coin easily and with certainty from a few paces off, beware the stranger bearing 3-legged nickels.

In Commemorative half dollars, there is a great price difference between the two 1922 issues of the Grant Memorial coin: $16 for the commoner; $130 for the rarer. The more valuable Grant has a star in the obverse field. So what could be simpler for the con man than to procure a star punch and oblige his customers?

Only one thing is wrong with this bit of skullduggery—when he punches his fake star into place, a flattened spot appears on the reverse of the coin. Thus, the wise collector scrutinizes a Grant with Star half dollar with extreme care —on both sides.

In the world of the phony, beware the coin which has been buffed to look like a Proof.

Proof coins are carefully struck under great pressure, using only specially polished planchets (or blanks). The result is a coin which, in addition to almost needle sharpness of detail throughout, has a mirror-like finish in the field (background).

Now, a buffed coin, at first glance, may look like a Proof. Under the magnifying glass, however, the needle-sharp detail is nowhere to be seen. There appear to be countless tiny scratches, and there's a peculiar glaze over all, that's not at all Prooflike.

Gold coins frequently are buffed in an attempt to make

them resemble Uncirculated or Proof coins. In every case, a reasonably good glass will show it is neither—even if you haven't learned to identify that peculiar glaze that buffing brings.

With the current craze for Proof sets, silver coins also have been buffed by get-rich-quick artists in an attempt to sell them at right smart, if not exorbitant, prices. Again, place reliance on a good glass before you fall for "Proofs" at bargain prices.

With all phonies, real or suspected, whether restrikes, doctored coins, or the silk-purse productions, own and learn to rely on a good magnifying glass. Don't be afraid to use it. A reputable dealer or fellow collector is flattered that you care enough to scan the very best.

CHAPTER NINE

# Proof Coins—
# the Dutch Bulb Era
# of Numismatics

## PROOF COINS—THE DUTCH BULB ERA
## OF NUMISMATICS

Familiar to every student of economics is the story of the great Dutch bulb mania which swept Europe a few centuries back.

No one appears to know for certain exactly how it started. Someone may have spread rumors that this particular tulip bulb was twice as rare as that; this one would produce a rare and exotic black tulip; another would flower into a fragile blossom which was unique in texture as well as color.

Almost immediately, intelligent persons who probably couldn't have distinguished a tulip from an aster started to buy these "rare" bulbs. Urged on by speculators and each other, the buyers saw the prices zoom skyward. A bulb that sold for a mere 100 guilders last week brought 1,000 this week—that lot of six exotic black tulip bulbs went for a mere 25,000 guilders—perhaps the price tomorrow would be nearer the 100,000 mark.

Then some doubting Thomas may have decided to plant the exotic bulb to see exactly what sort of a "rare" tulip would appear. Or perhaps some sane person merely stood back to take a long hard look at this Dutch bulb business. At any rate, the whole balloon of inflation suddenly collapsed—and tulip prices returned to their pre-mania level.

Present-day dealing in recent Proof sets may well be called the Dutch bulb era of numismatics. The rise and fall of fictitious values closely parallels the flower hysteria of a few centuries back.

Proof coins are those which are specially made at the

United States Mint in Philadelphia for presentation or sou-
venir purposes. They're minted much more slowly and
carefully than those in the regular production run. Perfect
planchets are selected, the dies specially polished, greater
pressure is used, and the entire process is more deliberate.

The result usually is a perfectly struck coin, with design
and lettering full and sharp. The surface of a Proof coin is
mirror-like and glitters distinctively.

The U. S. Mint has made such Proof coins for more than
a hundred years, including them in the official mint reports
from about 1860 for Indian cents and from 1863 for silver
coins.

But it wasn't until 1936 that mint officials decided to
issue them to the public as complete sets rather than individual coins. Such a set includes a cent, nickel, dime,
quarter and half dollar—total face value, 91 cents. The price
charged by the mint in 1936 was $1.81, with the extra 90
cents going to defray the additional costs of minting the
Proof coins.

In that first year, 1936, there were 3,837 complete Proof
sets minted and sold for $1.81 each. Coin collectors were
far from numerous and the demand was definitely small.
Fewer than 4,000 sets were deemed entirely adequate.

Through the years that followed, there developed something of a demand for the 1936 Proof set. Eleven years later,
in 1947, sets were advertised for sale at $59.50. That price
apparently was a little steep because, six years later, in
1953, the figure had slumped to $52.50 per set.

Starting about 1955, a large boom began to develop in
the Proof set area. The 1936 set (smallest total output of
the 1936–1942 period) soared spectacularly in price, reaching
a peak in the neighborhood of $750 about 1957. Speculators
and get-rich-quick experts were freely predicting that a
price of $1,000 was not far off.

Then came the Moment of Truth, which closely resembled the Dutch bulb blowup, when someone got off to one side and took a long hard look at the situation. From a peak of around $900, the 1936 Proof set hit the skids and didn't slow up until it neared the $250 mark, where it leveled off as an approximation of true value. The speculator who'd laid out $900 found his investment had shrunk to less than a third. He definitely was not too happy.

Proof sets of the years 1936 through 1942 are starting to climb back slowly in value, and the price for the 1936 set is in the neighborhood of $400 again. But it may be several years before it doubles to near its old-time high.

Minting of Proof sets was halted in 1942. After all, World Wall II was going full blast and "business as usual" was not the order of the day.

It should be remembered that the U. S. Mint is not in the business of money-making as a favor to coin collectors. To the mint, numismatists are just people, and occasionally somewhat difficult ones. The theory then was that Proof sets are made only if the mint is not behind on other business. Making of Proof sets can be discontinued at will—and has been on occasion.

The other chores performed by the U. S. Mint include the striking of medals for the services, medals of Presidents, Secretaries of the Treasury, and Directors of the Mint, as well as making coins for friendly governments.

Caught up on its work, the U. S. Mint resumed Proof set manufacture in 1950. Then, with the price of everything considerably above the 1942 level, the mint decided to charge a bit more for the sets—$2.10 for the five coins with the 91 cents face value. And the higher price is said to just cover the extra production costs.

In a few years, for reasons still obscure, the 1950 Proof sets zoomed upward in price. They were quoted at a higher price on the market than those of 1942, this despite the fact that there were 51,386 sets issued for the year 1950 as compared with a mere 21,120 in 1942.

It's quite true that the design of two coins had been changed; the so-called Mercury dime was replaced by the Roosevelt 10-cent piece, and the Walking Liberty half dollar had given away to the 50-cent piece bearing the portrait of Benjamin Franklin on one side and the Liberty Bell on the reverse.

But it is doubtful that these design changes improved the overall appearance of the Proof sets. In fact, there are those who consider both the dime and the half considerably inferior to the 1942 models.

An explanation occasionally advanced is that there are two stumbling blocks for the collector who'd complete the Proof series, 1936–1942, both 1936 and 1937 being priced beyond reach of the average collector. Yet the 1950 set goes merrily on its way toward the $100 mark, at which point it too may start to price itself beyond reach of Collector John Doe.

With the resumption of Proof coinage, sets which were issued in relatively modest quantities at the start showed surprising increases in value. From the original $2.10, the 1950 set advanced rapidly toward the $50 mark. Now, any item that can increase in value some 25 times in a few years is bound to attract attention. Even the stock market seldom offers stocks with such growth potential.

So, along about 1956, everyone decided to get into the act. Proof coinage totals had jumped from 51,386 in 1950 to 378,200 by 1955. The prices quoted for the 1955 sets didn't show the spectacular advances of the 1950, but they did double and triple the original cost of $2.10.

In 1956, the total Proof coinage nearly doubled that of the previous year, going to 669,384. And just about everyone thought it was high time he climbed aboard the band wagon.

Dealers, collectors, speculators, shoestring operators, and financial experts ordered Proof sets in 1957. They didn't just order 1 or 10 or 100—they shipped orders to the U. S. Mint running into the hundreds and thousands. These sets were tossed into safety deposit boxes by some, others were cached away in storage closets, and a few were actually bought by collectors who planned to display them.

Many dealers found that they had overbought. In the following year, the 1957 Proof sets were a glut on the market. The old economic law of supply and demand had gone into operation. Dealers who had tied up thousands of dollars in those glittering coins found they couldn't get their money out of them, much less make a profit. So, 1958 became the year of the Great Awakening—the apparent end of the Dutch bulb era of numismatics.

Dealers frantically sought to unload their surplus 1957 Proof sets. While they had put out $2.10, they sought buyers who'd pay as little as $1.75 for each 1957 set; dealers were content to take a loss just so their capital once more would be liquid and available.

The number of sets minted in 1958 (875,652) indicated a gradual return to near normalcy. The speculator, fingers burned, hesitated to go off the deep end that year.

The 1958 sets, being in relatively short supply, showed a surprising speculative rise in value. Illogical though it may appear, the 1958 set (with some 200,000 more minted) is actually quoted at a higher price than the 1956 set.

But the lure of the fast buck appears not to have been diminished to any great extent. In 1959, the total issue of Proof sets was 1,149,291; in 1960, the grand total was 1,691,602; in 1961, the issue reached an all-time high—3,028,244 sets.

Perhaps the Dutch bulb era isn't over yet.

# CHAPTER TEN

## The Designs on Coins

# THE DESIGNS ON COINS

Some 2,500 years ago, when metallic money was just beginning its long life as a medium of exchange, the metal in the coin itself represented full value. Thus, a gold coin was worth just as much as the gold itself was worth, a silver coin was worth no more nor less than its silver content, and so on.

Only one thing was lacking: a guarantee that the gold or silver was of standard purity and proper weight. The average person was not expected to carry along scales and assay equipment to prove or check the worth of this or that metal disk.

Ancient authorities sought to guarantee weight and purity by stamping into the coins a readily identifiable emblem or symbol or portrait. Thus, a rose with a bud meant that this particular silver didrachm had been issued by the Greek city of Rhodus on the Island of Rhodes; an owl and the Greek letters alpha, theta, epsilon indicated that the city of Athens guaranteed the weight and purity of the silver in its tetradrachm.

The Greeks were content at first to use portraits of gods and goddesses and mythological creatures—such as the Pegasus or flying horse, symbol of Corinth—on the obverse sides of their coins. This continued until the time of Alexander the Great of Macedon. During his world-conquering exploits (336–323 B.C.), Alexander issued silver coins which allegedly showed the head of young Hercules, or Herakles as he was called then, wearing a lionskin.

Now Alexander *said* that it was a picture of Hercules on

his coins, but those in the know whispered that Alexander himself had posed wearing the lionskin. So it may be said, with a degree of accuracy, that Alexander the Great was the first man in history whose portrait appeared on any coin.

The practice was continued with the rise of the Roman Empire. Coin engravers of the Empire usually were not as gifted artistically as the earlier Greeks, but they did their best. And the Caesars of Rome permitted them an unusual amount of unflattering accuracy—the portrait series of Emperor Nero shows him from handsome youth to fat middle age, with apparently little compromise with the truth.

Thus the designs of coins, whether symbols or portraits, were intended to assure whoever handled the money that he was getting more or less full value.

When the United States of America started its mint in the 1790s, the struggling new nation leaned over backward to make certain its coinage would be acceptable. The early large cents contained a full cent's worth of copper. In the case of the first silver dollars, the mint went slightly overboard and put more silver of greater purity into them than was necessary. They were, in fact, worth more melted down as silver than the dollar value stamped on them. Early gold coins also had too much, too fine gold in them.

Today, coins issued by the United States are more or less tokens, with no attempt to insure that a silver half dollar has 50 cents' worth of silver in it, or that a bronze Lincoln cent contains anything near one cent's worth of copper. But they are definitely legal tender—completely acceptable at full value by the American people.

In the early days of the American Republic, there were those who wanted the portrait of George Washington placed on United States coins. Despite many Washington pieces which appeared (many minted in England) during the period 1783–1795, the first President frowned on having his portrait used. Even as he declined to become "King" of the new nation, he refused to permit his likeness to appear on the new American coins.

(Not until more than 100 years later—in 1900—did the likeness of George Washington appear on an authorized United States coin. In that year, the Commemorative Lafayette dollar carried the conjoined portraits of Generals Washington and Lafayette.)

The first official production of the newly opened mint in 1793 was divided between half cents and the large copper cents. Exactly who designed these first coins is not known for certain, but it is believed that the half-cent design was a copy of the Saratoga-Yorktown medal made by the French artist Dupré.

There were two types of the 1793 large cent: the chain type and the wreath type. Dies for the chain design are said to have been cut by the Swiss artist Jean Pierre Droz. Public reaction to this first design was not at all friendly: "The American cents . . . do not answer our expectations." The chain on the reverse side met objections: "The chain . . . is but a bad omen for Liberty, and Liberty herself appears to be in a fright."

The wreath type of copper cent design of 1793 was probably cut by Joseph Wright, the first draftsman and die-sinker of the U. S. Mint, although it's possible that Droz suggested the design. The reverse bore a circular wreath instead of the objectionable linked chain, but Liberty appeared to be quite as frightened as before.

The next type of large cent, coined from 1793 to 1806, is called the Liberty Cap type, and the dies are believed to have been cut by Robert Scot, newly appointed first engraver of the mint.

This fellow Scot was probably the busiest and most prolific engraver ever employed by the U. S. Mint. Not only did he design the large cent but, starting in 1794, his designs appeared on the half cent, the half dime, half dollar and silver dollar.

Two years later, changes were ordered. (After all, the new mint was doing some experimenting.) For this series, Scot based his design on a portrait of Liberty by Gilbert Stuart, famed for his many oil paintings of Washington.

The new Scot designs appeared first on the dollar late in 1795 and on the large cent, half dime and half dollar in 1796. Two new silver coins were issued for the first time by the mint in 1796—both designed by Scot—the dime and the quarter. A new design for the half cent had to wait until 1800.

Gold Eagles and Half Eagles ($10 and $5 respectively) were first issued in 1795, and the Quarter Eagle or $2.50 gold piece appeared in 1796. All three were designed by Scot.

The Turban head large cent, 1808–1814, is so named because the broad ribbon with "Liberty" lettered thereon, plus the curled hair above it, has the vague appearance of a turban.

Concerning the so-called Indian Head cents, long a popular series with collectors, there is a legend which still persists. It is a pleasant story, possibly based on fact to an extent. Sarah Longacre, age 12, one day went to visit her father at the mint in Philadelphia. Her father, James B. Longacre, was then chief engraver. A small band of Indians and their chief were visiting the mint that day.

The chief is said to have permitted little Sarah to put on his feathered bonnet. So striking was the effect (the story goes) that Father Longacre sketched her portrait. He later used that sketch as a model for the famed Indian head which appears on United States cents from 1859 to 1909.

Designers of United States coins usually have included their initial or initials somewhere on the coin. Longacre may have been the first when he included a tiny letter "L" on the ribbon of part of the Indian Head cent issue of 1864. In doing so, he made a collector's item of those 1864 cents bearing his initial; the cent with the "L" is worth approximately 6 times as much as one without it.

Other coin designers have signed their work. Charles E. Barber parked his "B" on designs for dimes, quarters and halves of 1892–1916. George T. Morgan got away with placing an "M" on each side of the silver-dollar design of 1872–1921.

In 1907, Augustus St. Gaudens placed his monogram—ASG—under the date in his design for the Double Eagle ($20 gold piece), and Bela L. Pratt next year included "B L P" under the Indian's head on the Quarter Eagle and Half Eagle ($2.50 and $5 gold coins).

But Victor D. Brenner, who designed that favorite of so many collectors, the Lincoln Head cent, got into genuinely hot water when he sought to do likewise.

When the first Lincoln cents were issued in 1909, there appeared on the reverse three tiny letters: "V D B." Brenner was not prepared for the storm of protest that broke about his head. He was accused of advertising, braggadocio, impertinence, and so forth and so on.

The mints at Philadelphia and San Francisco were ordered to halt production of the new Lincoln cents until the offending initials could be removed. While Philadelphia had minted nearly 28 million of the V D B cents by that time, the San Francisco branch turned out only 484,000. Thus, the 1909-S with Brenner's initials on the reverse, is one of the key coins—and hence, most valuable—in the entire Lincoln cent series.

Federal law today says that the design of a coin cannot be changed oftener than once every 25 years. Thus, there are only two coins which are eligible for a new design: the Lincoln cent of 1909 and the Washington quarter, first issued in 1932. But there seems to be little inclination to abandon either.

A "new" Lincoln appeared in 1959, but the only thing new about it was a reverse side which featured the Lincoln Memorial in Washington, D.C. Thus far, there has been no hint that the Washington quarter will be replaced by a new design.

The Jefferson nickel design, adopted in 1938, became eligible for a change in 1963, but the Roosevelt dime (first issued in 1946) and the Ben Franklin half dollar (adopted in 1948) probably will be around at least until 1971 and 1973 respectively.

There are those who think the Roosevelt dime is a particularly unattractive coin, and they'd like to see it changed. But, no matter how unpopular a particular design proves, the mint is stuck with it. Unlike other manufacturers, who try to improve their product each year, the mint can't change models more often than once in 25 years, except by act of Congress. When a coin has been in issue longer than this, the Director of the Mint, with approval of the Secretary of the Treasury, may put out a new design.

Mint officials, unlike those in the Post Office Department, dislike coin-design changes. United States postage stamps may startle you with their bizarre colors and lackadaisical design, but a coin must be as familiar as an old shoe.

Once, in his message vetoing a bill which would have authorized a new commemorative coin, President Eisenhower said:

"Multiplicity of designs of United States coins would tend to create confusion among the public, and to facilitate counterfeiting."

(Of course, with the exception of Columbian half dollars, Stone Mountain halves and some of the Washington-Carver series, almost no commemorative coins ever reach actual circulation—they're fast gobbled up by dealers and collectors.)

There have been a number of two-design coins issued by the mint in the last hundred years or so; that is, coins which after the first issue were soon modified to some degree.

The Indian cent of 1859 underwent such a design modification on its reverse side. The following year, the original laurel had been replaced and an oak wreath with a small shield at top decorated the reverse side.

The Lincoln cent had only that minor change in its first year of issue—the removal of Victor D. Brenner's initials from the reverse side. While seemingly unimportant, the presence of those three initials on a 1909 Lincoln cent minted at San Francisco can add a whale of a lot of value to it from the collector's standpoint.

Restoration of the initials in 1918 was of no particular importance to the world of coin collectors, except it has often helped identify the 1944-D Lincoln which has been altered to resemble the more valuable 1914-D.

When the Lincoln Memorial reverse side, designed by Frank Gasparro, was introduced in 1959, a distinctively new series of Lincoln cents was started.

Those 5-cent pieces, familiarly called "nickels," actually have only a fourth part of nickel in their alloy—the other three parts are copper.

In World War II, when nickel was a critical item in the war economy, the alloy was changed materially. In the 5-cent pieces of 1942 through 1945, the alloy was 56 per cent copper, 35 per cent silver and 9 per cent manganese.

When the Liberty Head nickel first appeared in 1883, the word "Cents" was omitted from the design. In this first type, there was only a large Roman numeral "V" with no definite answer to "Five what?"

Dishonest persons (and there were such even in the 1880s) would have these nickels gold-plated and then pass them off to gullible rural characters as 5-dollar gold pieces. Of course, the weight wasn't right, but who's going to stop to weigh United States coins that "look" all right?

Because of this nineteenth-century racketeering in nickels, everyone seems to have saved that first type and promptly to have spent the nickels issued later in 1883, which had the word "Cents" prominently displayed on the reverse side of the coin.

The result is that today the 1883 nickel with "Cents" is worth from 4 to 6 times as much as the 1883 nickel without it. Despite rumors that ran regularly across the country, this 1883 centless nickel was never recalled by the U. S. Mint.

The next nickel was the Indian Head or Buffalo design, issued from 1913 to 1938. James E. Fraser was the designer. While at various times an Indian chief might come forward and stoutly declare and admit that he was the model for the design, Fraser actually used 3 different Indians as model—Irontail, Two Moons, and a Cheyenne chief.

The portrait of the bison, popularly miscalled a buffalo, has a more succinct history. A bison named "Black Diamond," in the New York Zoological Gardens, was the model here. A popular attraction for many years, "Black Diamond" passed on to the Happy Hunting Grounds in 1915. His head was preserved and mounted.

The Indian Head nickel underwent a minor revision in its very first year of issue. The bison first appeared standing on a mound on which was stamped the coin's value. But it wore out much too rapidly. The new type had a base redesigned to provide a thinner straight line, with a recessed area for the value.

The Standing Liberty quarter, issued in 1916 and for part of 1917, underwent considerable modification in that second year. Not only was the reverse side changed, but the obverse side underwent considerable modification—exactly why, no one appears to know.

In the original design, the figure of Liberty was tall and straight. A shield covered the left upper half of her body, but her right breast was bare. The new design modestly gave her a coat of mail. No one knows for sure, but it's a good guess that some bluenoses and do-gooders decided that the original design was "indecent." And everyone knows how a vociferous minority sometimes gets its way.

The real and legitimate drawback of the coin was that on the series 1916 through 1924, the dates wore off rapidly and completely. In 1925, part of the pedestal on which Liberty is standing was recessed. The coins dated 1925 through 1930 proved much more durable. In fact, the coins often were well into the "Fair" condition before the date became undecipherable.

It's possible that designers of United States coins are becoming so expert, or they think things through so well, or their designs are so safe and obvious, that changes are never required after the first coin appears. At any rate, there hasn't been a major change in any United States coin series since the Standing Liberty revamp of 1917.

# CHAPTER ELEVEN

## New Role for an Old Distillery

# NEW ROLE FOR AN OLD DISTILLERY

What could be done with an old distillery property? If the year was 1792? If the city was Philadelphia? Here's the story:

When David Rittenhouse was appointed by George Washington to be the first director of the United States Mint on April 14, 1792, it was considered an honor, a responsibility and a challenge.

Here was a brand new republic with no monetary system of its own; the United States was simply coasting along using various foreign coins. The Spanish 8 reales or "piece of 8" was the commonly accepted standard of value, although Dutch and English and German coins could be found among those in circulation.

However, that was not the biggest problem for the new mint director—he had no mint to direct!

So Mr. Rittenhouse started searching through Philadelphia, at that time the federal capital, for a likely place for his mint. He found some property that was fairly close to his home and not too far from President Washington's residence. It looked good and was certainly convenient. So he recommended its purchase and Washington okayed it.

The new mint site was the former home of an old Philadelphia distillery. Cost to the U.S. taxpapers—exactly $4,266.67.

The old buildings which had been used by the distillery weren't quite right for the manufacture of coins, so Congress came through with money for a new mint structure, the first cash ever appropriated for erection of a public building in the United States.

The first of three mint buildings, eventually erected on the old distillery site, was completed September 7, 1792. Later that month, workmen started on a somewhat hesitant production schedule.

Free coinage of silver was to be the policy of the United States. The new mint wasn't ready to start full-scale operations, but President Washington thought it ought to have a trial run at making some coins.

So, according to tradition, he bundled up some of the family silver and took it to the mint to be melted down and coined. There is no record of exactly what silverware he took along, but the items may have included some old candlesticks and snuffers, a battered berry spoon or two, and whatever other articles appeared not needed in the Washington household.

There's no way of knowing whether Martha Washington was consulted in what silverware could be spared. It's possible that the President decided to act first and tell her about it afterwards.

So, late in September or early October of 1792, there were coined some silver "half dismes." These were turned over to the President (after all, it *was* his silverware that went into them), and he distributed them to friends and relatives. It is said that the portrait on those first "half dismes" was of Martha Washington, although it is doubtful if she was flattered by the somewhat too plump representation.

In his fourth annual address to Congress, in October of that year, President Washington reported:

"There has been a small beginning of coinage of half dismes, the want of small coins in circulation calling the first attention to them."

The word "disme," current in 1792, stems by way of the

French from the Latin "decimus" or tenth. The pronunciation in those days was "deem." While it was spelled out on those very first half and full disme experimental coins of 1792, when regular full-scale operation of the mint was begun in 1794, no mention of value was made on either coin. The American of that day was presumed to know at a glance, by the size of the coin, which was which and worth how much.

Marks of value were left off the half dimes from 1794 through 1805. When coinage of this small silver piece was resumed in 1829, the value was expressed on the reverse side as "5 C." With the change of design in 1837, the original name of 1792 was resumed—half dime (without the "s" in the middle)—and it continued to be so designated until its career ended in 1873, 81 years later.

When the mint was ready to start business in 1792, Director Rittenhouse hired a watchman, hung a large bell in a tower in the mint yard, and bought a watchdog for $3 as protection for the mint.

There is no record as to the dog's name—it may have been Rover or Tige, Butch or Strongheart. But he was a good watchdog. And that $3 price tag is no guide to the dog's real worth; after all, Director Rittenhouse, considered America's topmost scientist of his day, drew only $2,000 a year as mint director.

There were certain rules which the dog and his friend, the watchman, followed. No one except the watchman was allowed to feed the dog. At night, when the mint was closed down, the watchman, armed with a pistol and short sword, was required to ring the yard bell every hour on the hour by the mint clock. And, after the bell had tolled out its message that all was well within the mint, the dog was turned loose to make his own private inspection of the premises.

The mint watchdogs, from that first one which cost $3

through all his successors, turned in perfect performances. Not once, from 1792 until the old mint was abandoned and sold in 1832, was there a successful break-in.

Mint employees in these early days turned in a full daily measure of work. They reported to the job at 5 A.M. and weren't through for the day until 8 P.M. There were no coffee breaks and they couldn't go out for breakfast, lunch, or dinner; they either carried their food with them to the job or depended on relatives and friends to bring meals to the mint.

Once on the job, no worker could leave the mint without permission. If caught outside the fence, he was considered to be guilty of a dishonorable act and was promptly stripped and searched. Few workers wandered outside.

The 15-hour day prevailed throughout the year. But there were two big holidays when the workers could stay home all day—the Fourth of July and Christmas Day.

Lighting in the mint buildings left something to be desired. There were plenty of tallow candles but only a few whale-oil lamps. Considering all this, it is remarkable that early American coins look as good as they do.

On several occasions, the mint had to be closed down for months at a time due to epidemics of yellow fever.

Power for the coin presses and other machinery was supplied exclusively by men and horses until 1816. Following a mint fire in January of that year, steam power for certain heavy work was introduced. But it was not until 1836 that true steam coinage finally got under way in the newly-opened second mint in Philadelphia.

In its act establishing the U. S. Mint, Congress ordered that on each gold and silver coin "there shall be the figure or representation of an eagle." That same act stated that on all copper coins the denomination of the piece be stated "cent or half cent, as the case may be." There was no such requirement for silver and gold, and the earliest American gold and many silver pieces curiously omit any statement of value.

No one knows what eagle or eagles posed for the required "figure or representation" on the reverse of America's earliest coins. But the bird that served as a model for the silver-dollar designs of 1836–1840 was a famous eagle called "Peter."

Why an eagle should select the U. S. Mint for his home isn't too clear, but Peter did so and lived there for some six years. Peter, considered a magnificent specimen of the American eagle, daily flew leisurely about the city of Philadelphia. But he never failed to come back to the mint building before it was closed for the night.

Christian Gobrecht had been appointed an assistant engraver at the U. S. Mint in 1836. Upon orders of the mint director, he set out to design some "pattern" dollars. In each case, the flying eagle on the reverse was a "representation" of Peter, the mint eagle.

The age of mechanization eventually proved Peter's undoing. He came to an untimely end after an unfortunate set-to with a flywheel. Exactly what happened is lost in the mists of history. One version is that Peter attempted to perch on the moving flywheel, another is that Peter tried to fly through the wheel while it was moving so rapidly that it was little more than a blur.

Whichever account is correct, America's most famous eagle did reach an unfortunate end. But Peter's career of service to his country was not closed then. The magnificent bird was stuffed and found a permanent home in a glass case in the mint collection room.

CHAPTER TWELVE

# What to Look For in Your Change

# WHAT TO LOOK FOR IN YOUR CHANGE

When a friend learns that you collect coins, about the first thing he or she will say is:

"What coins are you looking for? What are the good dates? I'll be glad to look over my change every day. Just tell me what you want and I'll save them for you."

About 2 out of every 5 such friends actually mean it— they will really try to help you round out your collection. The other three (if, for instance, you should happen to mention that a 1916-D dime is worth from $40 up) are likely to make a mental note that, if they should come across some "good" dates, they'll dash with them to the nearest coin dealer. Not that they mean to be dishonest or unhelpful, but, after all, didn't *they* find the coins and aren't *they* entitled to the profit, if any?

But, for those 2 friends who may really want to help you, these skeletonized lists may be useful. They are far from complete and are not intended to be a substitute for any good standard catalog of coin values.

First of all, realize that in the long series that goes back to the days of the Young Republic, there are three principal classifications into which coins can be put, so far as finding them in change:

1. Impossible.
2. Unlikely.
3. Possible.

For instance, what are the chances of finding either an

1877 or a 1909-S Indian-head cent in change these days?
They're well-nigh impossible.

Let's break it down. The chance of finding any Indian
Head cent in change today is about one in 100,000. So the
odds here are considered Unlikely. Then, once having hit
the jackpot and found an Indian cent, what are chances
that it'll be an 1877 or 1909-S? Possibly one in some
2,000,000. With these compounded odds, it's safe to call the
1877 "find" impossible.

The chance of finding a 1931-S Lincoln Head cent in
change is Unlikely, but far from Impossible. And the same
thing can be said for certain other lesser "key dates."

So let's go through the various series and classify them as
to chances of finding examples in circulation today.

HALF CENTS and LARGE COPPER CENTS. Impossible.

INDIAN HEAD CENTS (1864–1909). Unlikely.

But a friend may have an assortment of Indian cents he
inherited or that was put aside by his grandmother. What
are certain of those worth? The valuable ones (in Good
condition, the lowest collectible state) and the catalog
ranges might be listed:

INDIAN HEAD CENTS

| | | |
|---|---|---|
| 1877 | $47.50 to | $65.00 |
| 1871 | 13.00 to | 17.50 |
| 1872 | 16.00 to | 21.00 |
| 1908-S | 9.50 to | 11.50 |
| 1909-S | 45.00 to | 55.00 |

It must be remembered that these prices are those which
dealers will charge you for such coins in Good condition;
it does not mean they'll pay you that much for them. On
certain coins (usually the slower-moving ones), you may
get 50 per cent of catalog value, or even less. On the "keys"

such as the 1877 or 1909-S Indian cents, you may ask for and get as much as 80 per cent of catalog, possibly more. For a dealer knows that those key dates won't linger long in his display case. He undoubtedly will sell them within a day or so at full catalog or even a bit more. Since his turn-over is fast, he's willing to work on a smaller margin of profit.

In the Lincoln cent series, there are a half dozen key and semi-key dates. While theoretically, many of these are still in circulation, the chances of finding them might be called Unlikely. Such Lincoln cents and their retail values (in Good condition) are:

LINCOLN CENTS

| | | |
|---|---|---|
| 1909-S V D B | $50.00 to | $70.00 |
| 1909-S (plain) | 11.00 to | 15.00 |
| 1911-S | 3.50 to | 5.00 |
| 1914-D | 25.00 to | 32.50 |
| 1922 (plain) | 7.00 to | 12.50 |
| 1924-D | 3.00 to | 4.50 |
| 1931-S | 9.00 to | 12.50 |

A peculiarity of the Lincoln cents coined in 1931 at the San Francisco and Denver branch mints is that the 1931-D in Good condition has a catalog value of a mere dollar and a half, but in Uncirculated condition it's rated a $45 coin, or $2.50 higher than its Uncirculated brother from San Francisco.

One accident in the Lincoln series, the 1955 doubled-die cent, is quoted at from a hundred dollars or so in Extremely Fine to well over $200 in Uncirculated state. If you find one in circulation, you'll not have much difficulty indentifying it; you'll get the impression that someone stuttered badly when stamping the coin, particularly in the area of the date.

There are no 2-cent bronzes or 3-cent pieces (either nickel or silver) in circulation today, so you can cross those coins off as Impossible to find in change.

The shield type nickel 5-cent piece (1866–1883) is usually classified as Impossible.

Liberty Head nickels (1883 through 1912) are Unlikely but not Impossible. When you do encounter one in change, chances are that it will be so well-worn that it is a struggle to call its condition Good.

Valuable dates in Good condition:

LIBERTY HEAD NICKELS

| | |
|---|---|
| 1885 | $40.00 |
| 1886 | 20.00 |
| 1912-S | 15.00 |

Again, these are the retail selling prices which you can expect a dealer to charge you, not what the dealer will pay you. The other Liberty nickels in Good condition range in retail worth from 40 cents to a high of $4, with the majority in the lower price range.

Don't bother to search for a 1913 Liberty Head nickel, no matter what outfit advertises it will pay thousands of dollars for an example. They simply are not now and never were in circulation. There are 5 specimens known and all are accounted for. While produced in the mint, they were not officially issued by the mint.

Buffalo nickels (1913–1938) are still occasionally to be found in change. Often the date is worn to the point of doubt, if not extinction, and any mint mark has suffered a like fate. But sometimes a passable specimen will be encountered.

The price range for the better dates in Good condition:

## BUFFALO NICKELS

| | |
|---|---|
| 1913-S Var. I | $ 3.00 to $ 6.00 |
| 1913-S Var. II | 16.00 to 25.00 |
| 1913-D Var. II | 9.00 to 10.00 |
| 1915-S | 3.50 to 4.50 |
| 1918/17-D | 65.00 to 80.00 |
| 1921-S | 6.50 to 9.00 |
| 1924-S | 3.50 to 4.00 |
| 1925-D | 3.00 to 5.00 |
| 1937-D (3-legged) | 12.00 to 15.00 |

Half dimes are, of course, Impossible; they haven't circulated in the United States for many years, although their Canadian cousins were in use until about 30 years ago.

In the dime division, you're not likely to find any before the Liberty Head (Barber) type, starting in 1892 and continuing through 1916.

Good dates for this series in Good condition:

## LIBERTY HEAD DIMES

| | |
|---|---|
| 1892-S | $14.00 |
| 1894-O | 25.00 |
| 1895 | 20.00 |
| 1895-O | 40.00 |
| 1896-O | 16.00 |
| 1896-S | 25.00 |
| 1897-O | 17.50 |
| 1901-S | 17.50 |
| 1903-S | 7.50 |
| 1904-S | 7.00 |

In the Liberty Head series, the most valuable one you could find in circulation—the 1895-O—had a total issue of only 440,000. Each coin on the list had a total minting of under one million, so, even if you're very lucky, you'll probably not encounter one every week or even every year.

Others have been looking for those desirable dates for some 60 years plus.

The next series is the Winged Head Liberty (best-known as Mercury Head) dime. Despite the fact that the head looks very much like that of the Mercury of mythology, the designer said he intended the wings crowning the cap to symbolize liberty of thought.

Coins in this series, which started in 1916 and continued through 1945, are currently to be found in circulation, often in better than Good condition. Thus far it is an underrated series which may be due for a real boom one of these years.

The ones to look for, even in Good condition, are:

MERCURY DIMES
(Winged Head Liberty)

| | | |
|---|---|---|
| 1916-D | $47.50 to | $55.00 |
| 1921 | 4.00 to | 5.00 |
| 1921-D | 5.00 to | 8.00 |
| 1942/1 | 37.50 to | 40.00 |

The 1942-over-1 overdate is one of only a few to have occurred in modern United States coinage. It has been located in recent years with considerably greater frequency than the 1916-D.

The short-lived United States 20-cent piece, issued only from 1875 through 1878, naturally belongs in the Impossible category.

Early quarter dollars can be classified as Impossible, while those of the Seated Liberty type, starting in 1838 and continuing with modifications through 1891, are most Unlikely.

Occasionally Barber quarters (1892 through 1916) are encountered in change. Almost without exception they are well-worn, and few manage to have enough design left to qualify as in Good condition. But there's always the chance that some valuable Barber quarters will get into circulation quite by accident. So here's the lookout list:

BARBER QUARTERS

| | |
|---|---|
| 1892-S | $ 9.00 |
| 1896-S | 47.50 |
| 1897-O | 6.50 |
| 1897-S | 7.50 |
| 1899-S | 5.50 |
| 1901-O | 8.00 |
| 1901-S | 130.00 |
| 1904-O | 5.50 |
| 1909-O | 10.00 |
| 1913-S | 55.00 |

The 1901-S quarter is rated at $130 for one very good reason—there were only 72,664 of them minted. Yet the 1913-S, which is even rarer from the standpoint of total made (40,000), catalogs a mere $55.

Standing Liberty quarters (1916–30) still may be encountered in change. Unfortunately, most of them are so far gone that the dates are practically obliterated, even though a mint mark (when present) can be made out.

But, if you should come across a Standing Liberty or two, here are the "good" dates and their values in Good condition:

STANDING LIBERTY QUARTERS

| | | |
|---|---|---|
| 1916 | $100.00 to | $125.00 |
| 1918/7-S | 75.00 to | 125.00 |
| 1919-D | 12.00 to | 17.50 |
| 1919-S | 18.00 to | 20.00 |
| 1920-D | 7.00 to | 8.00 |
| 1921 | 11.00 to | 12.00 |
| 1923-S | 20.00 to | 24.00 |
| 1927-S | 5.00 to | 6.00 |

There are many who believe that the Standing Liberty quarter, when well-struck and in Uncirculated condition, is one of America's most beautiful silver coins. Sometime you might stop in at a coin shop and ask to see an Uncirculated example. Don't be surprised if you are captivated by the coin's beauty and possibly decide to make this series your specialty. But, be warned: it's one of the most difficult (hence expensive) series to put together in Gem Uncirculated condition.

The Washington quarters (starting in 1932) are regularly encountered in change. There are only two dates that thus far have any premium value in Good condition, the 1932-D ($5) and the 1932-S ($3). All the rest must be Fine or better to be worth much over face value, and most must be Uncirculated.

Very early half dollars—from 1794 through about 1840—are Impossible to find in change. The Seated Liberty type, starting in 1839 and continuing through 1891, is Unlikely. But, if you should happen to encounter one, here are the good dates and their catalog values in Good condition:

### SEATED LIBERTY HALF DOLLARS

| | |
|---|---|
| 1866-S (no motto) | $ 35.00 |
| 1870-CC | 50.00 |
| 1871-CC | 30.00 |
| 1873-CC (no arrows) | 30.00 |
| 1873-CC (arrows at date) | 20.00 |
| 1874-CC | 25.00 |
| 1878-S | 240.00 |
| 1878-CC | 80.00 |
| 1872-CC | 27.50 |

The CC halves were made at the branch mint in Carson City, Nevada. They were produced in relatively small numbers (only 62,000 in 1878), and they apparently were worn out rapidly in the rip-roaring days of the old West. The San

Francisco half dollar of 1878 commands a fine, fat premium because the total made in that year was only 12,000.

Seated Liberty half dollars, dated from 1879 through 1890, are most difficult to locate and vastly underpriced in almost every catalog. Here was a series (minted only in Philadelphia) where the total each year ranged from a low of 4,400 in 1882 to a high of only 12,000 annually for the three "big" years of 1888, 1889, and 1890.

Now, the average coin catalog says that, in Good condition, these are worth from $11 to $21 each. But try to buy them from dealers in any condition except Proof. For some reason, Proofs of these dates are relatively easy to find offered for sale, with catalog prices ranging from $60 for the 1879 (1,100 made) to $100 for the 1886 Proof (886 minted).

Barber half dollars (1892 through 1915) are to be found from time to time in change. Most of those which are still circulating are well-worn and don't make the grade of Good. Here are some of the better dates and mint marks to look out for:

### BARBER HALF DOLLARS

| | |
|---|---|
| 1892-O | $20.00 |
| 1892-S | 20.00 |
| 1893-S | 19.00 |
| 1896-S | 20.00 |
| 1897-O | 20.00 |
| 1897-S | 19.00 |
| 1901-S | 6.00 |
| 1904-S | 6.00 |
| 1913 | 7.50 |
| 1914 | 7.50 |
| 1915 | 9.00 |

Barber half dollars in lesser condition currently are not in hot demand. So, don't be surprised if the dealer isn't interested in buying your coins for more than about a third of catalog. He knows they'll be in his display case for quite some time before a customer for them comes along.

Walking Liberty halves (1916–1947) are still circulating, and one can put together a complete set without too much difficulty. The key dates you should look for, and their price range in Good condition:

### WALKING LIBERTY HALF DOLLARS

| | |
|---|---|
| 1916-S | $7.50 to $10.00 |
| 1917-S (on obverse side) | 4.50 to 5.00 |
| 1921 | 6.50 to 8.50 |
| 1921-D | 6.50 to 8.50 |

Only two Franklin halves (series starting in 1948) are worth premiums in less than absolutely Uncirculated condition. In Extremely Fine condition, the two dates and their catalog values are 1948 (95 cents) and 1949 ($3). All other dates in this series must be Uncirculated to have any value above the face value.

The moral of all this appears to be that a person can have a lot of fun building a good collection of United States coins in the current and recent series through daily inspection of his pocket change. But his chances of finding really rare and valuable coins among such change are dim indeed—the rarities appear simply to have been removed from circulation.

CHAPTER THIRTEEN

# Unusual Coins of
# the United States

# UNUSUAL COINS OF THE UNITED STATES

Long before the days of the sales tax, that well-worked source of revenue in so many states, there were some unusual American coin denominations that would have come in quite handy in paying exact sales tax percentages. Unfortunately, most of them were discontinued about a hundred years ago, and there appears to be no move under way to revive them.

How convenient it would be, for example, if the half cent were still around. There would be no argument then about paying, say, the 3 per cent tax on a 15-cent purchase— a half-cent copper would cover it quite adequately. And, under the same tax schedule, the state collection on a 50-cent purchase would be exactly one cent and one half cent.

But the half cent of the United States joined the dodo bird in extinction away back in 1857.

This half cent was designed to meet the needs of a day when a full day's labor might bring in as much as a whole dollar. It was a time of strict economy in government, in stores and in the home, and Ben Franklin's advice—"A penny saved is a penny earned"—was followed religiously. The evening newspaper might cost all of a half cent, although a real sport might toss a full one-cent copper to the newsboy on the corner and grandly proclaim, "Keep the change!"

But there is a lack of popularity about the half cent today. The series hasn't caught on with collectors, and the commoner dates still can be purchased at reasonable prices. Of course, there are some stoppers in the series, and the collector who insists on a complete set of dates should have a rather fat wallet.

In its 64-year lifetime (from 1793 through 1857), there were fewer than 8½ million copper half cents struck and issued by the mint. In each of a dozen years, fewer than 100,000 were struck. The top total mintage was in 1809, when the mint reported it struck only 1,154,572 half cents. Compared to modern mint totals, this figure can be considered peanuts.

An unusual coin with a 9-year life span was the 2-cent bronze piece. First issued in 1864, it had one distinction—on it appeared for the first time the motto "In God We Trust." Its appearance is said to have been due principally to increased religious feeling during the Civil War. But the coin did not catch on with the public and it was discontinued in 1873.

Two types of 3-cent pieces have been minted by the United States—one in silver, the other in nickel. This unusual denomination is said to have been coined for the convenience of postal clerks. Three cents was the amount needed to post a letter during the period, and these coins were intended to keep postal change-making to a minimum.

The silver 3-cent piece, the smallest coin ever made by the United States, was first issued in 1851. The last regular minting was in 1862, although Proofs were continued through 1873. There are three types: the first (1851 through 1853) had no lines bordering the 6-pointed star, the second (1854 through 1858) had three outlines to the star, while the final type (1859–1873) had two outlines.

Best dates are the 1851-O, the only 3-cent piece minted in New Orleans, and the 1855 from the Philadelphia mint. From the standpoint of total made, the 1855 is much rarer than the 1851-O—139,000 compared to 720,000. Yet the catalog values in Fine condition are identical, and relatively close in both Good and Uncirculated.

The 3-cent nickel piece (1865–1889) is a series which offers little to the imaginative collector: there was only the one type issued, and the only thing to break the monotony in a complete set is the difference in dates. In its first year of existence (1865), there were issued more than 11 million nickel 3-centers—almost half again as many coins as make up the half-cent entire lifetime total.

A silver United States half dime, while it might appear strange in circulation today, actually was not an unusual coin for the America of 150 years ago. It was needed by thrifty housewives and careful merchants, and it was more than a mere token coin; it actually contained a half dime's worth of silver. Today's 5-cent nickel piece has taken its place, but the metallic worth of this coin is nowhere near its stated value.

Another weird denomination (by present-day standards) was the 20-cent piece, started in 1875, and abruptly phased out only three years later. The main trouble with the coin was that it looked much too much like a quarter dollar then current—and its size was too close.

A complete collection of 20-centers would include exactly seven examples, but it would be quite valuable. The 1876 20-cent piece struck at Carson City has a catalog value of around $7,000. The Carson City mint reported that it struck 10,000 of these coins in 1876, but most of them were melted down and never released. There are presently 14 such 1876-CC 20-cent pieces known.

An unusual coin was issued by the United States Mint in 1873—the Trade Dollar. It was not intended for circulation in this country but for trade with Japan and other nations in the Orient. The object in issuing it was to compete, if possible, with the silver dollars of Mexico and Spain, and to encourage the shipment of United States silver to the East Indies, for the United States had suddenly become a silver-producing nation.

For three years, the Trade Dollar was legal tender in the United States to the extent of $5 worth. But in 1876, this legal-tender provision was repealed by Congress (due to the decline in the price of silver bullion), and the Treasury was ordered to limit coinage to export demand.

There's long been a slang saying in this country: "As phony as a $4 bill." And, if you should tell a friend that you had a $4 gold piece in your collection, he'd figure you were either a bit balmy or were pulling his leg.

But the United States did once have a $4 gold coin. And, if you happen to have an example in your collection, you're a very lucky person, for its current catalog value ranges between $5,000 and $13,500.

Actually, the $4 gold piece, popularly known as a "Stella" because of the large 5-pointed star that dominates the reverse side, was a pattern coin. Yet it is one of the most popular of all United States coins.

It was issued in extremely limited quantities in Proof only—a total of 425 in 1879 and only 25 in 1880, the second and final year of issue. The least valuable Stella is the "Flowing Hair" type, designed by Charles E. Barber and issued in 1879. Its catalog value is a mere $5,750, while the "Coiled Hair" type, designed by George T. Morgan, is quoted at $13,500, providing the date is 1880. The Barber type of that year (1880) isn't too far behind, being valued at $11,000 in Proof condition.

This high-priced Stella has what might be called a "poor relation" in the gold coin family—the $3 gold piece. Even the existence of a $3 coin of gold often comes as a surprise to the average American.

But even this "poor relation" can command a high price if the date is right. For example, the 1875 $3 gold piece, of which only 20 were struck in Proof, is rated a $12,500 coin, while that of the following year (total mintage 45) is valued at $4,350.

The $3 gold piece was first issued in 1854 and continued through 1889. But it was never a popular coin with the public, and saw very little actual circulation.

Until a few years ago, even coin collectors didn't care too much for it. One could buy an Uncirculated example for less than $50. But all that changed abruptly. Today, most dates in Very Fine condition are cataloged from $150 upwards. In Uncirculated condition, the least expensive ones are cataloged at $200, with certain dates rated as high as $950.

And so, the unusual coins of the United States, having served the purposes for which they were intended, have vanished along with the oxcart, the oil lamp, and sulfur and molasses.

The 3-cent piece no longer is needed since it's not enough to buy one first-class postage stamp. Nor is the $3 gold piece sufficient to buy a hundred of those postage stamps.

The half cent could have been revived to good purpose when the sales tax first appeared on the state scenes. But it's too late now; the American public is accustomed to the 1-cent overpayment here and there.

The 2-cent copper, while popular and acceptable in its day, would be a pain in the pocket because of its size and weight today.

There's absolutely no need for a Trade Dollar. The American public can't even be persuaded to accept the lighter, standard silver dollar, except in areas where they'll fit slot machines.

But the unusual coins which the United States has issued over the years at last are finding homes in which they are appreciated—almost every collector appears to hope to get at least one of each type for his collection.

CHAPTER FOURTEEN

# U. S. Commemorative Coins

# U. S. COMMEMORATIVE COINS

As the name indicates, Commemorative coins were issued by the United States Mint by specific order of Congress at various times to celebrate some special occasion or event of importance. As such, they are considered an integral and important part of the history of this nation.

They have ranged in denomination from the 25-cent Isabella quarter, issued in 1893 by the Board of Lady Managers of the Columbian Exposition, to the $50 gold pieces, both round and octagonal, put out by the San Francisco branch mint in 1915 to commemorate the Panama-Pacific Exposition in that city. And their present values range from a few dollars for the commoner commemoratives to well over $4,000 for the round Pan-Pacific gold slug.

In a sense, commemoratives should be included among the Unusual Coins of the United States, for, although they are spendable, full legal tender, they seldom have been seen by the general public. With a few exceptions, these coins have never been in general circulation; many were sold at prices above face value; and generally they have been kept bright and shiny, just as they came from the mint.

The history of United States Commemoratives starts in 1892 with issuance of the Chicago Columbian Exposition half dollar, and ends rather abruptly 62 years later with the minting of the last of the Washington-Carver half dollars in 1954. In those 62 years, many important historic events were commemorated, as well as some of definitely dubious import.

The prices of Commemorative coins have had a somewhat spotted career. From the collector's standpoint, they alternately blow hot and cold. Currently, they're on the hot side. Indications are they'll stay that way. But, if history repeats, they may cool off without much warning and stagnate for months on end.

There have been gold Commemoratives, ranging in size and denomination from the tiny $1 gold pieces (Louisiana Purchase, Lewis and Clark, Pan-Pacific, McKinley Memorial, and Grant Memorial) through the $2.50 gold pieces (Pan-Pacific, and Philadelphia Sesquicentennial) to the heavy $50 gold slugs of the Panama-Pacific Exposition. And there have been the Isabella quarter and the Lafayette silver dollar.

But by far the largest number of Commemorative coins have been half dollars.

In complete contrast to the government's view on postage stamp issues, Secretaries of the Treasury and Presidents have frowned on Commemorative coins. While the Post Office Department will issue a special stamp almost at the drop of a hat, the Treasury Department dislikes to issue coins which vary in the least from those which have become familiar to the American public through day-to-day purchases. A special stamp may be issued which looks like a refugee from a bottle of patent medicine, but few persons squawk. The stamp collectors are delighted that they have a new issue on which to spend their money. And the government takes in quite a bit of cash through such sales.

Commemorative coins, however, are minted only when specifically authorized by Congress. The original idea was to issue these coins to organizations which needed them for fund-raising purposes in connection with more or less historic celebrations. Thus, a 50-cent piece might be sold by the Commemorative Commission for a dollar, the 50-cent profit going for some worthy project, such as sculpturing a mountainside or paying the costs of a centennial celebration.

All too often, the commissions yielded to the opportunity offered by coin dealers to unload quantities of their coins. It was a much faster way of meeting expenses than selling them one at a time to collectors. The dealers, in business to make a living, of course, then peddled the coins to collectors for whatever they could get—sometimes quite a fancy increase over the original price. Before long, there arose an unpleasant aroma.

Secretaries of the Treasury, from Andrew Mellon on, tried to call a halt to the practice. By 1937, when the 76th Congress adopted H. R. Report No. 101, the thing was considered to have become something of a racket, with coin dealers about the only beneficiaries.

That 1937 House action effectively put a stop to Commemorative issues until, on the final day of the 1946 session, a pair of bills slipped through. One was to authorize an issue of half dollars to commemorate the 100th anniversary of Iowa's admission to the Union, the other to aid the Booker T. Washington Birthplace Memorial.

Today, Commemorative issues do not easily get through Congress; and, when they do, they're vetoed by the President of the United States. President Eisenhower, during his two terms, vetoed three such bills.

So it appears that coin collectors will have to struggle along with the half hundred or so different types of Commemoratives that have been minted in the last 70 years. The type set collector of Commemorative half dollars need worry about only 48 types. If he's ambitious and wants all the mint marks and specials (Grant with Star, Missouri 2★4, etc.) his goal will be 142 coins and he'll have to put out well over several thousand dollars to complete the full set.

As to the artistic merit of the various Commemoratives,

there are many different opinions. Some contend that almost all these coins are not well designed. Others claim their historic importance far outweighs artistic considerations. Some think the lettering and legends required by law to be included (denomination, United States of America, In God We Trust, E Pluribus Unum, etc.), make it impossible to design a simple and attractive coin. And there are many who are quite happy with the design and appearance of practically all the Commemorative half dollars.

In the last 15 years, many of these Commemoratives have shown startling price increases, some justified on the basis of heavy demand for a limited supply of coins. Others appear to have been overtouted and the prices elevated beyond what normally might be expected on a pure supply-and-demand basis.

In such cases, a dealer may find he has to move certain examples below the figures that enthusiastic boosters of Commemoratives have wishfully hoped for. However, through the years, like almost all items in the coin market, Commemoratives appear to have had their values adjusted in accordance with sound economic laws.

A few of the better-known Commemoratives and their prices of 15 years ago as compared with today's average market:

### COMMEMORATIVE COINS

| Coin and Year of Issue | 15 Years Ago | Present |
|---|---|---|
| Isabella quarter (1893) | $ 7.50 | $ 65 to 75 |
| Lafayette dollar (1900) | 10.00 | 75 to 100 |
| HALF DOLLARS: | | |
| Columbian Exposition (1892) | 1.25 | 5 to 6 |
| Panama-Pacific Expos. (1915) | 17.50 | 70 to 75 |
| Missouri Centennial (2★4) (1921) | 35.00 | 110 to 135 |
| Vermont Sesquicent. (1921) | 4.50 | 37 to 50 |
| Hawaiian Sesquicent. (1929) | 27.50 | 335 to 460 |

## COMMEMORATIVE COINS

| Coin and Year of Issue | 15 Years Ago | Present |
|---|---|---|
| Old Spanish Trail (1935) | $12.50 | $150 to 200 |
| Battle of Antietam (1937) | 4.50 | 55 to 95 |
| New Rochelle, N.Y. (1938) | 3.50 | 50 to 80 |

Portraits of living Americans have appeared on Commemorative half dollars (no living American has ever been portrayed on coins of regular mint issue). Thomas E. Kilby, governor of Alabama during that state's centennial celebration in 1920, appears on the Alabama Centennial half dollar of 1921. It was the first time in history that a living person's portrait was used on a United States coin.

In 1926, during the Sesquicentennial of American Independence, the portrait of President Calvin Coolidge appeared with that of George Washington on the Commemorative half dollar. This was another first: the first time a portrait of a president had been used on a coin struck during his lifetime.

Senator Carter Glass of Virginia, former Secretary of the Treasury, objected to the idea of using portraits of living men on coins. But he was overruled and his portrait appeared on the obverse side of the Commemorative half dollar issued for the Lynchburg, Virginia, Sesquicentennial in 1936.

In addition to the American eagle, Commemoratives have portrayed various birds and animals. Among those pictured are the California grizzly bear, a calf, beaver, catamount, badger, Texas longhorn steer, oxen, horses, owls, and dolphins.

Depicted on other coins are such bits of Americana as a gold prospector of 1849, an Indian warrior, Hawaiian native chief, pioneer settlers, the first white child born in America, and a Panama Canal laborer.

There have been plenty of ships: Columbus' flagship *Santa Maria,* the Pilgrims' *Mayflower,* the *Half Moon* of Henry Hudson, and numerous other sailing vessels with identities more or less certain.

Battles commemorated are a pair from the Revolutionary War—Lexington and Concord—and two from the Civil War —Antietam and Gettysburg.

Designers of the Commemorative coins have not been without a sense of humor: there's the picture of "one fatte calf" required to be given each year by the early settlers of what is now New Rochelle, New York, and a solemn portrait of that distinguished American showman, Phineas T. Barnum, who is credited with the saying, "There's a sucker born every minute." There's even a pun on the Old Spanish Trail Commemorative—the explorer Cabeza de Vaca being represented not by a portrait but by a translation of his name, "head of a cow."

So, if you should decide that you simply must have a complete set of Commemorative half dollars, be prepared to spend in the neighborhood of $2,500 or more. Should you aim for the complete collection of 142 coins, you'd best double that estimate.

The wise collector, however, does not insist on completeness in Commemoratives or in any other series. He intelligently buys and saves those coins which appeal to him. And certainly there are many moderately-priced Commemoratives which are quite as attractive as those with top prices.

CHAPTER FIFTEEN

# Collecting and Investing and Speculating

# COLLECTING AND INVESTING AND SPECULATING

In the world of numismatics today, there are three main classes: the coin collector, the investor and the speculator. There is something to be said for all three, although most legitimate collectors are inclined to take a very dim view of the speculators.

## The Collector

If you become a collector, there are certain rules which you can make for yourself and follow. These rules are generally considered sound, although you may choose to modify some and ignore others.

FIRST RULE: Buy only those coins which please *you*. Since this is your hobby, those coins which can give you pleasure are those you should acquire. If you can take genuine pleasure in the coins you collect, you'll be happy. If you act principally on the advice of this dealer or that acquaintance, you may get coins which, once in your collection, will make you wonder why you ever put out any money, no matter how much or how little, for them. If, on the other hand, you bought a coin because its design or patina or overall appearance pleased you at that time, chances are excellent that it will continue to please you well into the future.

SECOND RULE: Buy single coins. Don't be tempted to purchase a completed series, because then a great deal of the fun of collecting is lost. If you want only a single specimen of a series, such as a silver 3-cent piece, don't be persuaded that you should buy a dozen or two just because you can get them for a little less per coin. You'll find the extra 11 or 23 are just so much excess baggage.

THIRD REASONABLY SOUND RULE: Either buy the best you can afford, or those coins which you consider the most attractive, or both. As in all things, quality is a consideration not to be taken lightly. It's usually better to have one coin in Extremely Fine condition than two or three Very Good specimens. You'll take greater pleasure in your collection if the coins, whether 2 or 200, are in a beautiful state of preservation.

At first, if you're like most collectors, you'll go in for quantity rather than quality. But, as you become more experienced, you'll want to replace the inferior coins with better examples. And you may decide to discard many which merely are so-called "space fillers." It's something like the old adage, "One bad apple can spoil the whole barrel"—one inferior coin may detract from the striking appearance of all the others.

FOURTH RULE (WHICH IT'S A GOOD IDEA TO FOLLOW): Be catholic in your taste. At the outset you may decide to accumulate coins regardless of series until you can decide which coins you desire to concentrate on and *collect*.

So you give up accumulating and become a collector. But, once having decided upon an era or series, don't become so engrossed in your specialty that you overlook or neglect other beautiful coins. The type collector might be considered the prime example of one with catholic taste; he wants a fine specimen of every type of half cent, half dime, large cent or half dollar, and he's not interested in any one series. He has fun, the same as any other collector, so who's to deny him his type collection?

The well-rounded collector is usually the person who has finally found a series he likes, is concentrating on it, but does not close his mind to acquiring a type coin here and there if it pleases him.

FIFTH RULE: Don't be frightened by a price tag, or be impressed by it. Some coins in Extremely Fine or Uncirculated condition may carry what appears to be an unusually high price. If the coin pleases you, fits in somehow with your collection and your pocketbook can afford it, don't be frightened away. By the same token, don't hurry to purchase a coin merely because the price *is* high. Don't be persuaded by the seller. Make certain that the coin pleases *you* and that it will bring a measure of pleasure proportionate to its cost. If it fails to measure up to the standards you set for yourself and your coins, pass it up.

SIXTH GOOD RULE: Avoid "junk," even though it may fill a blank space in your collection. As mentioned previously, you'll be a happy collector if you learn to live with blank spaces. Maybe you'll be able to fill them properly. Meanwhile, forget them and be not unhappy.

An example of the extreme to which a type set collector might have to go if he couldn't live without a blank space is in the album page labeled "Types of U. S. Half Dollars." There are spaces for 9 types, starting with 1794–1795 and continuing through 1916–1947. Now, eight of those spaces can be filled with passable examples (Good or better) for from a few dollars to a maximum of about $65 for a Good 1795. But that ninth space, Type 2, 1796–1797, must be filled by a Good example for a minimum of $700.

Is there any collector (except one to whom money is absolutely no object) who would be willing to pay about $700 for a single coin in a series in which the other 8 examples cost altogether only $100 or so?

One collector solved the problem by cutting out a halftone picture of a 1797 half dollar, mounting it on a circular piece of corrugated board, and inserting the picture neatly into the blank space. If a friend inquires why there's only a picture instead of a coin in that opening, the collector honestly reports he didn't care to spend $700 just to make the page complete.

SEVENTH RULE, WHICH A WISE COLLECTOR MIGHT FOLLOW: Study carefully the early United States coins—they're the classics of American numismatics. True, you'll never encounter a half-cent piece or a bust-type half dollar in change, but you'll get a whale of a lot of pleasure and satisfaction if you put together one of the early United States series.

EIGHTH AND FINAL FACT OF A COLLECTOR'S LIFE: If you have followed the first seven rules, and there comes a time when you have to part with your coin collection, the chances are excellent that you'll realize a profit on what you've spent, even though you've made no conscious effort to plan it that way. Fine coins, particularly the early ones, appear to increase in value annually. The reason is rather obvious: there simply are not enough to go around.

## The Investor

Suppose you decide to invest in coins. Are there any rules which you might follow? While not exactly rules, there are suggestions which it might prove wise to heed. But they are not any more guaranteed to make you money than is the advice from your Wall Street broker.

The wise investor is guided somewhat by mint totals. The early reports are vague at best, for the simple reason that the mint reported how many coins of a certain denomination it *issued* during a certain year, not how many were actually *struck* in that year. Thus the mint reported it put out 19,570 silver dollars in 1804 (and there are about 14 more or less authentic examples known today) and that same year issued 156,519 silver half dollars (of which not a single example is known today).

The second suggestion for one who would invest in coins:

Look carefully into the neglected series—the half cents, half dimes, silver 3-cent pieces and bust-type half dollars.

The half-cent series has been discussed at length previously. Of principal significance is the fact that the total output of United States half cents was only slightly more than 8 million coins, and that most of these available today are underpriced in comparison with large cents and other early United States coins.

Half dimes from 1829 through 1873 are still reasonably priced. The earlier examples—1794 through 1805—with their higher prices due to rarity, are believed to be the only drawback to a real boom in half-dime collecting. But when enough collectors will be content to leave unfilled those spaces prior to 1829, expect the half-dime series to show real growth in values.

Most silver 3-cent pieces have reasonable price tags, principally because the last 11 years of issue were minted in Proof only. Again, if the blank spaces from 1863 through 1873 can be ignored, this series may catch on.

Bust-type half dollars dated from 1807 through 1836 long were a drug on the market. Until a few years ago, a collector could get every date (with exception of 1815) in Fine condition for around $5 or less. Today, the values are up considerably. That same series in Fine condition would range from a minimum of $4.50 for the least expensive example to around $20 for the scarcest example. In Uncirculated condition, the price increases have been spectacular—it was discovered that there simply aren't many Uncirculated examples around any more.

The third suggestion for the investor is to buy the best coins available. This means the best of the earlier coins, not recently minted specimens of "scarce" coins, on which someone attempts to put an artificial value, though there may have been as many as 2 to 5 million minted.

There's some question whether an investor should buy the

very best coin—for instance, a "unique example." If he does purchase such a treasure, he may not be able to dispose of it (at a profit or any other figure) unless and until he finds someone who simply must have the very best. If he's in coin buying to make some money, he's much better off with choice Extremely Fine or Uncirculated coins, for there are usually enough of them around to reflect demand and supply.

The fourth suggestion is one which should be obvious: Don't try to corner the market on any specific coin—it can't be done. Earlier issues are too well dispersed to permit it, and recent coins have been issued in such quantities that an investor would have to hire a warehouse just to store his hoard.

## The Speculator

In recent years, many persons have decided that rolls of modern Uncirculated coins will be valuable some day; that is, have a value above that stated on the coin. Possibly they will, but probably not until every American suddenly decides to become an avid coin collector, thus creating a demand for coins minted annually by the many millions.

Such roll collectors are in the forefront of the speculators. Now, there are some speculators who have made a specialty of attempting to corner all the $3 gold pieces in sight, and others try to monopolize certain dates in the Standing Liberty quarter series, but the vast majority are those who buy and trade and sell rolls of Uncirculated recent coins.

Now, some coin rolls conceivably could be very much worthwhile—such as a roll of 1795 dollars—except that no one ever collects genuine scarcities or rarities that way.

These strange hoarders of current coins barter rolls as if they were bars of silver or gold or platinum. They swap among themselves and create a strange sort of make-believe market in which prices can go up and down with the speed of a first-rate roller coaster. Occasionally, some sharp hoarder decides he's had enough of this strange hysteria and proceeds to unload his accumulation. The crash that follows sounds a lot louder than the boom which preceded. And numbers of innocents have been burned by this strange mania for trying to get rich quick through rolled coins.

Of course, saving some rolls of Uncirculated coins as they are issued is of manifest value to the collectors of tomorrow. But who should get into this act of being savior to the numismatists yet unborn? Should it be the reputable dealers? And who decides who is reputable? Should it be every Tom, Dick and Harry with an urge to get rich quick?

Which rolls should be saved? And how many? Can there be any reasonable prophecy of scarcity for a cent with a total year's mintage of around 250 million? Such a roll, with a face value of exactly 50 cents, today is bounced back and forth between roll dealers and roll collectors until the quoted theoretical value may reach $2 or $5 or even more. Such silly bartering of modern common coins, even though they be in the best of Uncirculated condition, often arouses the disgust of the more-or-less normal coin collector.

Occasionally, you'll hear a true history of the spectacular rise in price of a roll of legitimately scarce coins. For example, back in 1947, a dealer bought several rolls of 1931-S Lincoln cents at $20 a roll. Now, this date is a key coin in the Lincoln series, with total mintage of only 866,000.

One week later, the dealer sold them at $25 a roll. About 6 months afterward he was able to buy them back and promptly sold them for $50 a roll. Nine years later, in 1956, he bought one of those same rolls (they'd gone through the hands of 4 or 5 others meanwhile) for $400 and sold it the next day to a collector for $425. Today, such a roll is worth in the neighborhood of $2,000.

It is on such stories as this that the mania for roll collecting is based. The speculators aren't concerned with scarce issues (such as the 1931-S with mint total of only 866,000) but they tout each other on the advisability of tying up lots of good money in rolls of half dollars (total mintage over 5 million), quarters (5 to 10 million per year), and nickels (with a mint total of more than 2½ million). And these are all modern coins, issued within the last 20 years. How long will it take such coins to become even moderate scarcities? That's the jackpot question.

With the roll-collecting mania there has sprung into existence the so-called "suitcase dealer." He has a post-office box as his business address, and usually engages in his coin speculating as a side line. His stock may be great, but it's usually rather small. His expenses are at an absolute minimum. Despite all this he calls himself a coin dealer. He may advertise his buying and selling prices. But, unless he has a firm order from a cash customer to buy, he often will decline to buy your coins because he's "overstocked" at the moment.

Proof sets comprise another area which has experienced the blight of the speculator—the fellow who'd get wealthy without using either brawn or brain. The spectacular rise (and subsequent fall) of the 1936 United States Proof set can be credited with starting it all. This set, issued by the U. S. Mint in 1936 for a total charge of $1.81, zoomed skyward in the middle 1950s and reached the neighborhood of $750 before it hit the skids. Now, anyone who can build a $2 investment into hundreds of dollars in about 20 years is bound to have a lot of imitators. Even the fact that the skidding 1936 set eventually reached a sub-peak level of around $250–$300 didn't bother the easy-money lads.

So, led by speculators, the rush for United States Proof sets was on in earnest by 1957. From total Proof set mintings ranging from 3,387 to 21,120 in the period 1936 through 1942, the modern Proof sets zoomed to a total of 1,247,952 in 1957. The market was glutted and the quoted price fell as low as $1.85 each—30 cents under the cost at the mint.

The following year there was an indication of a return to sanity; a mere 875,652 were minted in 1958. Result? The 1958 Proof set now has a quoted value that's higher than the 1956 issue, which had a total of 669,384 made. Perhaps there's some logical explanation of this phenomenon, but it escapes the average rational American.

It is reported that conservative institutions, such as life insurance companies, and sane individuals, such as lawyers and bankers, have put aside hundreds, even thousands of these Proof sets. Have they hopes of spectacular increases in value? Could there be another reason?

One final phenomenon of numismatics today is the issuing of various and sundry medals by reputable firms as well as by the speculators. This medal mania undoubtedly was started by someone to fill the void left in the Commemorative coin area when Congress and Presidents frowned on further Commemorative issues.

The new medals appear to be issued for almost any occasion, from the planting of the first peanut in the South to the launching of the largest showboat on the Mississippi River. They seem to have one thing in common: to make money for the firm or individual issuing it. They are struck in almost every metal imaginable—alloys of various kinds, silver and even platinum—but not gold. The government still takes a dim view of such a use for gold.

What's the future of this rash of medals? Who can guess?

Of the three types presently in the world of numismatics —the collector, investor and speculator—it would appear that the knowledgeable collector, who buys good coins which please him, stands as good or possibly even a better chance of coming out ahead financially in the long run.

And there's always that intangible but valuable item, the pleasure and relaxation he gets from his hobby. Sometimes that's almost as good, possibly even a little better, than just grubbing for an extra buck or two.

8      3/1/88